Home Is Where God Sends You

Home
Is Where
GOD
Sends You

Lessons in Contentment from
Nearby and Faraway

Janet Benlien Reeves

ISBN-13: 978-1481921640
ISBN-10: 1481921649

To the One who always leads us home

Contents

Introduction

If you ask a military kid where he or she comes from, chances are you'll get a blank stare. My oldest left for college as we were settling into a new home. Since then, he tells people he's from the US of A. At that time, he also told me he was pretty sure he'd become homeless and would be for those next four years.

"Home is where your mommy is," I told him, confidently.

He smiled. "Can I quote you on that?"

It soon became obvious that my college-bound son wasn't the only one confused about our family's definition of home. When we arrived at new student orientation to deliver him to school, I was given a name badge that said I was from Belton, Texas. It took all I had not to scribble that out. I fought the urge for hours. It wasn't that I had anything against Belton, Texas. I liked that town just fine. But I'd only lived there for two months and calling it home just didn't feel right.

Complicating things was the fact that I had attended that same college. Being there kinda felt like being home, but the powers that be said it wasn't home for me. They defined Belton as my home. I did not like that.

Toward evening my husband asked me why I was so quiet.

"I'm still trying to decide if I should scribble out Belton or not."

"Why?" he asked.

"They've misdefined me," I said.

"Or maybe you've misdefined yourself."

I decided I'd have to think about that. Eventually, I decided he was right.

Some say, "Home is where your heart is." That may be true, but only if your heart is where God is which is everywhere at once and anywhere you are and all the places He sends you. That doesn't clear things up much, though.

For me, the simplest definition is: Home is where God sends me. This is true whether I'm living among people who speak another language or close to people I've known all my life. The sooner I accept this, wherever I go, the sooner I'm content and able to serve my Lord.

Chapter 1
Getting the News

Do You Not Know?

"Do you not know? Have you not heard? The Lord is the
everlasting God, the Creator of the ends of the earth. He will not
grow tired or weary, and his understanding no one can fathom."
–Isaiah 40:28

God created the ends of the earth. What a coincidence! That's where you're going! At least it's where you think you are going. Wherever it is, God created it. That being true, you now have something to look forward to. Imagine it's your birthday. God has many surprises for you! What will He pack into your new home? He's the only One who knows—but you're about to find out.

Will the adventure be too much for you? God never tires, but He knows that you do. As a loving parent carries a weary toddler, God will carry you. He'll introduce new experiences and opportunities at a pace you can handle, and He'll give you the strength you need to do all He's planned for you (verse 29).

You won't always understand God's ways (why you're moving, why your house won't sell, why the house you want is no longer available, why life doesn't go your way), but you'll always know you can trust God's understanding when you reach the limit of yours (and hopefully, before). God created the ends of the earth—and He wants to share their delights with you.

Everlasting God, I'm ready to see what You've planned for me. Since You're the Creator, I know it's good. Amen.

Bold, Not Terrified

"Have I not commanded you? Be strong and courageous. Do not be afraid; do not be discouraged, for the Lord your God will be with you wherever you go." –Joshua 1:9

"We're moving to the Netherlands! Who moves to the Netherlands? WHERE is the Netherlands?" Needless to say, this destination surprised us. Back-to-Southern-California was the place we'd hoped for, prayed for—all right, set our hearts on. But . . . the Netherlands . . .? ("Isn't that somewhere near Holland?" I'd asked.)

Earlier moves to Maine and New York had seemed pretty adventurous to this West Coast girl. I'd reluctantly learned to shovel snow—and to wait for the snowplow man to pass before I *began* shoveling snow. Now I'd have to learn a new language.

Each of our children had a different reaction to the news: Four-year-old Seth was too little to remember our last move, so he didn't quite understand what we were up to. Alex, three years older, remembered, and didn't want to move again—ever! Justin, our oldest, was up for adventure but felt leaving the country was a little much. Mike and I weren't sure just *what* to expect. But on the day the news came, our new-every-morning computer desktop background brought up a scenic picture with Joshua 1:9 as the caption. I don't remember the picture, but I'll never forget the verse: "Be strong! Be courageous! God is going with you *wherever* you go!" (Paraphrase mine.) Even to the Netherlands!

Joshua 1:9 became our theme verse for that move. We printed it in big letters and hung it on a kitchen cabinet. We memorized it, discussed it, and prayed about it. Driving from New York to Arizona and California to say good-bye to family and friends, we claimed it as a personal promise. Finally, as we took that giant leap in a jet plane to *our* new Promised Land, we allowed it to help us trust God with whatever giants we'd meet.

Father, thank You for being with us wherever we go. Help us obey Your command to be strong and courageous as Joshua did. Remove the terror and discouragement from our hearts and lead us boldly into our new land. Amen.

By Faith

*"By faith Abraham, when called to go to a place he would later
receive as his inheritance, obeyed and went, even though he did
not know where he was going. By faith he made his home in the
promised land like a stranger in a foreign country; he lived in tents,
as did Isaac and Jacob, who were heirs with him of the same
promise. For he was looking forward to the city with foundations,
whose architect and builder is God."* –Hebrews 11:8-10

Can you relate to Abraham? Have you obeyed and gone even
when you didn't know where? Have you lived as a stranger in a foreign
country? Have you and your offspring lived in tents—not camped in
tents, but really *lived* in tents? And *we* think moving is a challenge!

God said, "Go!" and Abraham went. The Bible doesn't say God
spoke to Sarah, but she went, too, leaving family, friends, and the only
life she ever knew. People question our family's sanity when we move to
a new place without first finding a home. Abraham and Sarah moved
without picking a location! Imagine saying to your family, "We're moving
tomorrow. God wants us to go. We don't know where, but we'll write
and let you know when we get there." Abraham and Sarah trusted God
to pick the place in a foreign country among strangers. No wonder we
find them in Hebrews 11, known as the chapter on *faith*.

Why did Abraham and Sarah obey? According to Hebrews 11:10,
they were "looking forward to the city with foundations, whose architect
and builder is God." Sounds like Heaven to me. As you face the
uncertainty of yet another move, leave the details to God like Abraham
and Sarah did. He's already picked the place. More importantly, He's

leading you to your permanent home. Trust Him with each stop along the way.

Master Architect, Builder, and Real Estate Guide, I'll trust you with the details of each move I face. Thank You for each home You provide. Amen.

Step One: Pray

"How gracious he will be when you cry for help! As soon as he hears, he will answer you." –Isaiah 30:19

All right! You're moving. The location is determined (hopefully). Your house is on the market. The movers are scheduled to come. Life as you know it is coming to an end.

Before you begin pulling pictures off the walls and calling friends to say, "Good-bye," though, take time to make the first step in this move the right step. Take some time to pray. Take *lots* of time to pray.

God already knows you are moving. He knew this was coming before you or your spouse or the employer who is sending you or hiring you or anyone else knew. He knows the fact. He understands your situation better than you do, but He wants to be included in the event.

So invite Him to come along. In fact, invite Him to be in charge. Welcome His guidance and help as you will welcome the movers who come to wrap every individual piece of your great-grandmother's china to keep it from breaking, so that you don't have to. God *wants* to lighten your load. He *wants* to assure you you're on the right track. He *wants* to encourage you through this whole moving process in every little way.

Take the time right now to take the first step. Get down on your knees. Pour out your heart. God hears you. He loves you. So pray.

Lord, bless my family as we face this move. Come with us. Help us. Show us the way. Open the right doors at the right time and lead us through each one. You're in charge, God. We'll do this Your way. Amen.

Trying

"And God is able to bless you abundantly, so that in all things at all times, having all that you need, you will abound in every good work."–2 Corinthians 9:8

I'd be lying if I said moving came easy for me, that I always look forward to and enjoy the adventure. I try to enjoy the adventure, but the truth is moving is a lot of work. It takes a long time to prepare. It takes a long time to settle in. It takes a long time to make friends and understand the workings of a new community. And about the time I feel comfortable in my new place, it's time to start over again.

Sometimes I'm tempted to complain. Sometimes I even yield to the temptation. But complaining doesn't make the situation any better. In fact, as I complain, I only feel worse. Frustration and discontentment build inside until everything begins to look bad. Next, my family begins to catch my bad attitude, and soon, we're all grumping at each other and at everything we see. Complaining doesn't fix anything.

Thankfully, God does. With grace, He gives me everything I need to do what needs to be done—even a good attitude. As I do my part to help my family move from point A to point B, the work is good. Given a task to complete and a challenge to meet, I can rely on God to help me succeed with determination and a smile. Then my cheerful example can encourage my family. God blesses us all abundantly when we look to Him for help.

Father, graciously give me the attitude I need to do good in all things at all times. I need Your help to make the difference. Thank You for the opportunity. Amen.

Broken or Crushed

"The Lord is close to the brokenhearted and saves those who are crushed in spirit." –Psalm 34:18

Recently, a friend's husband was informed that his position at the company he'd served for years was being eliminated. Not only did he lose his job, but also his company-provided home—the family was given a mere sixty days to locate themselves somewhere else.

How did they respond? At first they struggled with grief, frustration, confusion, and fear. Yet they quickly began to fight these enemies, calling on close friends to join them in prayer. Before the sixty days were gone, their confidence had returned. Further, he'd found a better job, close to extended family and requiring fewer hours and less travel. They'd also found a new home, and they gave God *all* the praise. As we said good-bye to these precious friends, we marveled at God's provision and care. When their spirits were crushed, God was certainly there.

Downsizing. Distance. Divorce. Death. When circumstances spiral out of control leaving your broken heart amongst the wreckage of the incomprehensible, turn *to* God, not away, for the comfort, courage, and wisdom you need to move on.

How can you do this? Start by sitting in silence and praising Him for His presence. Whether you sense Him or not, He is there! Next read His Word daily to find personal messages addressed just to you for this time. God's Spirit has an astonishing way of hiding them there. Don't forget to invite friends to join you in prayer when possible. God can comfort you through them, and they'll rejoice with you when it all turns around! Most important of all, believe these Bible-proclaimed facts: the Lord is close, and He *will* save.

Father, broken hearts and crushed spirits hurt. Thank You for coming close. I cling to Your promise to save. Amen.

Always the Same

"Jesus Christ is the same yesterday and today and forever."
–Hebrews 13:8

As I lay in bed the night before I left for college, I prayed, "Lord, after tomorrow, my life will never be the same." Those words had more truth to them than my experience at that time could grasp, and I've included that sentence in my prayers many times since—the night before my wedding, the night my first child was born, the night before each new move. In fact, I'm praying them now for myself and for each of my children as each, in turn, leaves home to face whatever his future holds.

The prayer is a simple statement of fact. Life is changing. And because life is changing, it is time to thank the Lord for all that came before and to commit to Him all that will come after. This is why Hebrews 13:8 is such a comfort. The world is changing all the time, but Jesus doesn't. Jesus has faithfully carried me through everything my past has held. Therefore, I can trust Him with my future, too. Jesus loves me—He will always love me. Jesus is in control—He will always be in control. Jesus is with me—He will never leave. He keeps His promises. In an unstable world with surprises around every turn, Jesus is steady and stable. Jesus is always the same.

After today, Jesus, my life will never be the same. I don't even know what this coming tomorrow holds. But I know You are with me, and You will never change. Thank You, Lord! Amen.

God Is in Control

"So we say with confidence, 'The Lord is my helper; I will not be afraid. What can mere mortals do to me?'" –Hebrews 13:6

I'm going to let you in on a little secret. Shhh! Don't tell! Whenever our employers send us to a new assignment, they do so with God's blessing. They may or may not realize this, but God won't let them send us anywhere that He doesn't want us to go. Shhh! Don't tell. It's our secret!

That secret, however, gives us confidence whenever we face a move. We don't have any reason to fear—even when someone calls to say, "Congratulations! You're going to (fill in the name of the most unlikely place you can imagine)!"

I was listening to my husband's side of the conversation when that call came to our home in Maine. We were hoping for Arizona, California, or even Colorado—somewhere closer to our families on the *West Coast*. Our God has a sense of humor. New York is closer, but not by much.

As my husband talked to the chaplain on the phone, he wrote *New York* on a piece of paper and pointed to it. I decided that meant we had to drive *through* New York to get wherever we were really going. Surely we weren't moving to New York. (We'd prayerfully requested California, after all!)

When Mike got off the phone and patiently explained that we really were moving to the Empire State, I wanted to know who was responsible for such an absurd choice. To my surprise, God raised his hand. I'm pretty sure He had a mischievous smirk on His face. It wasn't a malicious smirk—God loves me too much for practical jokes. But He knew what our future held: adventures, struggles, deep lessons, and life-long friends. Though unanticipated, the time had come for us to move to New York, and God couldn't wait to reveal His perfect plan.

As we begin to submit choices for each new assignment, I can now look back on the outcome of that experience with confidence and pray:

Lord, You are my helper; I will not be afraid. I'll entrust my future to You. Amen.

Disappointed or Devastated?

"Create in me a pure heart, O God, and renew a steadfast spirit within me . . . Restore to me the joy of your salvation and grant me a willing spirit, to sustain me." –Psalm 51:10, 12

When we learned we'd be moving from Maine to New York, I was disappointed. I had hoped to move much farther west. Without a willing spirit, however, I'd probably have been devastated. A willing spirit is essential to a successful and happy move.

Psalm 51 records David's confession after his affair with Bathsheba and the arranged murder of her husband. The prophet Nathan confronted David's sin in a manner that forced him to see what a wicked thing he'd done. (See 2 Samuel 12.) David threw himself on God's mercy and let God do what was necessary to restore David's soul. Whenever I realize that things between God and me aren't quite right, I turn to Psalm 51 for guidance.

Feeling devastated by a move is such a time. Devastation comes when we refuse to move past disappointment into acceptance. If you are feeling this way, ask God to give you a pure heart and a steadfast spirit. Are you upset because the move isn't going according to your plan? Ask God to show you *His* plan, and steadfastly determine to follow wherever that plan says to go. Are you unwilling to adapt to a new community or culture? Ask God to fix that, too. A willing-to-do-whatever-God-says spirit will sustain you no matter what the circumstances are. Disappointment is okay, but devastation is not. Turn to God and He'll provide the Spirit you need to make this move.

Father, with Your help and a willing attitude, I discovered there's a lot to like in Watertown, New York. Thank You for turning disappointments into good friends and happy memories. Amen.

Jonathan's Example

"Jonathan said to David, 'Go in peace, for we have sworn friendship with each other in the name of the Lord, saying, "The Lord is witness between you and me, and between your descendants and my descendants forever."' Then David left, and Jonathan went back to the town." –1 Samuel 20:42

In 1 Samuel 20:31, King Saul tells his son Jonathan, heir apparent to the throne of Israel, "As long as the son of Jesse lives on this earth, neither you nor your kingdom will be established. Now send and bring him to me, for he must die." Both Saul and his son knew that God had chosen David to be the next king. Saul reacted by pursuing David with the intent to kill. Jonathan, on the other hand, humbly helped David escape.

I wonder what Jonathan was thinking as he made the decision that would guarantee the fall of his family's royal line. As a child, had Jonathan *dreamed* of becoming king? How could he lay aside that dream for someone else? Did he want the job? Or did his father's poor example cause him to view the position with disdain? He surely knew that in order for David to take his place, he'd have to die. It was, after all, the custom of the day. The Bible records Jonathan's natural concern about this: In verse 14 of the same chapter, Jonathan asks David to show him kindness that he may not be killed. Ultimately, he was killed, but it wasn't David who did the deed. And in fact, David kept his promise to show kindness to Jonathan's family once he did become king.

No matter how Jonathan wrestled with these issues, one thing, apparently, never caused him any internal strife. Jonathan was committed to letting David be the next king no matter what. God's will was clear, so he honored both his friend and his God.

Likewise, when God calls us to change our plans or lay aside our dreams or start all over again in unfamiliar place, we can fight like Saul—

15

and discover frustration and futility. Or we can humbly follow Jonathan's example and trust that God will always lead the right people to the right place. God is in control, and He loves us. We can trust His ways.

Wise Father, Your way is best, even when I don't understand. I submit to You. Amen.

Submission

"'I am the Lord's servant,' Mary answered. 'May your word to me be fulfilled.'" –Luke 1:38

Time and again in the Bible, we read the responses of God's people to His commands. When God told Moses to go to Egypt, for example, Moses argued and argued and argued some more. God had to send Moses' brother, Aaron, to help before Moses agreed to obey. (See Exodus 3:1-4:17.)

When God told Jonah to go to Nineveh, Jonah said, "No way, Lord! Not me!" Then, even after the unforgettable fish experience, Jonah had the nerve to criticize God's ways. (See the book of Jonah for this story.)

When God sent Ananias to open Saul's eyes, Ananias expressed fear. He felt certain God was sending him to his death. (See Acts 9:13.) Even Peter questioned God soon after, refusing to eat unclean animals at God's command. (See Acts 10:14.)

I guess it's only human to question what one doesn't understand. Thankfully, God was patient with these people and graciously used them to accomplish His purposes in spite of their hesitant ways.

True submission, however, means obedience *without* the questions. Mary didn't understand how God's plan for her life could possibly work out. In fact, her assignment was probably the most unlikely of all. But Mary accepted the assignment right away. No "Send someone else," "No way," or "Are You sure You know what You're doing, Lord?" from her. Simply, "I'm your servant. Let it happen as You say." Mary's response is an example of perfect trust, pure love, and due respect for the God who deserves it. No wonder God chose her to bear His Son!

Father, questions are human, but You are worthy of better. With Your Spirit's help, I'll try to say, "Yes," to whatever You ask of me. Amen.

Thank You, Lord

"Let us come before him with thanksgiving." –Psalm 95:2

What can I be thankful for when facing a move? As I approach God's throne through prayer, I thank Him for the opportunity to move out of my comfort zone and into something that will challenge me to grow. I thank Him for new friends, scenery, and weather patterns. I thank God for an adventure that forces me to cling to Him for help every moment. I thank Him for the close bond that moving brings to our family. I thank Him for new ministry and service opportunities. I thank God that sorting, throwing away, and organizing are essential; when I move, most clutter stays behind. I thank God that I never have time to become bored with one place.

What does your thanksgiving list look like? It may differ dramatically from mine, though some elements will be the same. This doesn't matter. What matters is that you recognize God's gifts and thank Him for them. God wants to hear your concerns about each move, but He also wants your thanksgiving—when you enter His throne room through prayer, present the thanksgiving list first. God loves and cares for you; He deserves your humble thanks!

Gracious Father, thank You for all the good that comes with each move. Thank You for strength, confidence, family, and friends. Thank You for Your presence, most of all. Amen.

Seen By God

"For the eyes of the Lord range throughout the earth to strengthen those whose hearts are fully committed to him."
−2 Chronicles 16:9

When I read this verse, two Bible characters immediately come to mind: Noah and Job. We find Noah's story first, in Genesis 6-9. In chapter 6, verse 7 we learn that God has decided to wipe mankind from the earth. Verse 8, however, says that, "Noah found favor in the eyes of the Lord." God's eyes found a man who was fully committed to Him. As a result, Noah and his family were spared. They had to find a new home somewhere on the mountains of Ararat (See Genesis 8:4.), but they lived to tell the story. I'm certain Noah never forgot how serious God is about total commitment to Him.

Later, we read about Job in *his* book. In chapter 1, verse 8 God speaks to Satan, "Have you considered my servant Job? There is no one on earth like him; he is blameless and upright, a man who fears God and shuns evil." While it's true that Job lost everything as result of that conversation, he came through his trial with a greater respect for God, a stronger commitment, and double the blessings with which he began. (See Job 42.)

When God sees your devotion to Him, when He knows you'll remain faithful no matter what comes, God will use the circumstances of your life, whatever they are, to strengthen you. The strength He gives will carry you through life's trials and prepare you for eternity with your loving Lord. What a blessing to be seen!

Here I am, God! Look at me! Please give me strength for all that lies ahead with You! Amen.

No Surprises

"From one man he made all the nations, that they should inhabit the whole earth; and he marked out their appointed times in history and the boundaries of their lands." –Acts 17:26

Tracing my family's history is one of my hobbies. I first started this search for my roots because I wanted to learn which country my ancestors came from. Since my maiden name is Benlien, I grew up believing that most of my family, on my father's side at least, came from Germany. I was very surprised to learn that Germany plays a very small role in my ancestry. In spite of the name, most of my ancestors come from England, Ireland, and Denmark with a few Bavarians, Prussians, Welshmen and a Native American or two thrown in to keep the study interesting.

Some family lines are easy to trace. The family came to America, settled in one community, and stayed put until someone married someone who brought a branch of the family to California where I was born. Other family lines have been impossible. The family came to America from who knows where and moved from one place to another to another until the path back in time and across the seas was lost to researchers like me. (I'm carefully recording all of our moves now, in thoughtful consideration of my someday-to-be-frustrated descendants.)

What amazes me most about family history, however, is the fact that if even one of these ancestors of mine had lived in a different place at a different time, *I* wouldn't be here today. God carefully chose the time and place for each of their lives to begin, and He also chose the time and place for mine. I may not understand the many transitions of my life, but God does—and He has a purpose for each.

Wise Lord of All, I choose to trust You through each transition of my life. I may not understand them, but I believe You determined them in the best interest of Your kingdom. Your Word says that You marked out the time and the places of my life. I will not complain. Amen.

Remembering Ittai

"But Ittai replied to the king, 'As surely as the Lord lives, and as my lord the king lives, wherever my lord the king may be, whether it means life or death, there will your servant be.'" –2 Samuel 15:21

David was on the run again. Saul was long gone, and David had been king for many years. But now David's son Absalom wanted to be king—and he didn't want to sit around to wait for David to die. He was taking matters into his own hands, and David was running for his life.

Among David's faithful followers was a Gittite named Ittai. When David remembered that Ittai was a foreigner, he encouraged him to return to safety with others from his country. Ittai refused. His pledge to David reminds me of Ruth's pledge to Naomi. (See Ruth 1:16-17.) Both David and Naomi urged people they cared about to take the easy way out of a tough situation. Both Ittai and Ruth offered their faithful support instead.

Likewise you may be called upon to sacrifice the security of your home "country" in support of someone you love. When your husband's job takes you somewhere you don't want to go, you have a choice to make. You can gripe and complain every step of the way, making the whole family miserable and refusing to allow anything positive to come of the change. You can remove all support and refuse to go, effectively breaking up the team—perhaps permanently. Or you can put one hand in God's hand, the other in your spouse's, and bravely go on to face whatever the future holds.

Father, the thought of moving to some places frightens me. Help me to learn a lesson from Ittai, though. Wherever You want me, wherever my husband may be, that's where I want to be, too. Amen.

Moving As an Act of Worship

"Therefore, I urge you, brothers and sisters, in view of God's mercy, to offer your bodies as a living sacrifice, holy and pleasing to God—this is your true and proper worship." –Romans 12:1

Have you ever considered the possibility that moving can be an act of worship? You may not enjoy the prospect of uprooting and transplanting your family without your close friends, but you know it is what God is asking of you at this time. If that is the case, you are following Paul's urging and offering a living sacrifice. In obedience to Christ, you are placing your life in His hands and trusting Him with the outcome. This is holy and pleasing to God. It's an act of worship because trusting God with every aspect of your life, allowing Him to rule as He has the right to, is the most effective way to glorify His name. A successful transition requires this kind of trust.

What are you offering Christ today? He doesn't want your house or your friends or your favorite restaurant or your money. "The earth is the Lord's, and everything in it, the world, and all who live in it" (Psalm 24:1). Christ wants your life, given freely for His use, no strings attached—or tying you down. Doesn't He deserve what only you can give?

Lord, I offer my life to You. Place me where you will. Use me as You will—for the glory of Your name and growth of Your kingdom. Amen.

Gypsies

"You open your hand and satisfy the desires of every living thing."
–Psalm 145:16

My grandmother used to call herself a frustrated gypsy. Except for ten years in Northern California, she lived her whole life in Southern California. She lived in the same house with the pretty white picket fence for many years, dreaming of visits to exotic places. Even in her eighties, she still enjoyed road trips, camping, and visiting friends and family. It was impossible to keep her down for long. Sometimes it seemed she craved my moving-every-few-years life.

What she didn't know was that I'm a frustrated gypsy, too. Sometimes this mover longs for the permanent house with the white picket fence. I've lived within driving distance of the Eiffel Tower, but I wonder what it would have been like to live in one neighborhood long enough to truly get to know one's neighbors and watch each other's kids grow up.

As I think about this, though, I don't think either my grandmother or I truly wanted to trade places. Grandma loved living near her children and, well, *almost* all of her grand- and great, grandchildren. And if I had stayed put, I probably would always have wondered what would have happened if I'd gone. God called us to our respective lives. In Him, we're satisfied.

Father, when I'm tempted to play the "what if" game, remind me that You are in charge. I've given my life to You, and I trust You to lead me and my family along the most satisfying path to our future in Heaven with You. Thank You, Lord! Amen.

Milk and Honey

"If the Lord is pleased with us, he will lead us into that land, a land flowing with milk and honey, and will give it to us."
–Numbers 14:8

When preparing for a move, I try to learn all the positive things I can about the place where I'm going. I look for the "milk and honey" as Moses encouraged the Israelites to do. But I'm careful not to paint a picture in my mind that my new home can't possibly live up to. That would only assure my disappointment. My goal is to realistically accentuate the positive.

As we packed for the Netherlands, well-meaning people told us all kinds of horror stories about what we'd find in such an ultra-liberal country. News stories were scandalous, and yes, they presented us with issues of genuine concern for a conservative Christian family. We weren't ignorant of these elements of the society we'd be entering, but rather than fear them and dread the move, we turned these over to God, trusting Him to protect our family from their influence. That done we were able to look forward to tasting Gouda cheese, seeing tulips in the Springtime, chasing windmills, learning a new language, and meeting the fascinating people of a unique culture.

If the Israelites had done the same, they'd have entered the Promised Land forty years earlier. When they did claim the land, they found both milk and honey *and* giants, just as we found in the Netherlands. With God's help, however, the giants flee—and the honey tastes oh so sweet! Once you entrust your future to God, you can boldly go where He directs. He'll give the Promised Land to you.

Keeper of My Soul, I place my family in your care as I eagerly look toward the good in each new experience You lead us into. Amen.

Chapter 2
Packing Up Your Treasures

God's Loving Work

"My eyes will watch over them for their good, and I will bring them back to this land. I will build them up and not tear them down; I will plant them and not uproot them. I will give them a heart to know me, that I am the Lord." –Jeremiah 24:6-7

When we move from one community to another, we tear everything down and uproot our families. Such violent words! Yet they accurately describe the feelings that go with the actions. Packing is a hurried and harried process; sometimes it seems we are literally tearing pictures off the wall and throwing them into boxes in the rush to get out of the house. If we've lived somewhere a while, I often feel like I'm pulling long stringy, clingy roots out of the ground one by one in my efforts to go. I carefully pull all the roots I can in order to take them along, but some refuse to let go of the soil. These must be cut off and left behind. Tearing down and uprooting is a painful process for all.

Jeremiah 24:6-7 is full of God's promises for those who face this though. God promises to watch over His people *for their good!* He promises to take them to the Promised Land someday. In the waiting time, God promises to build His people up. (After tearing down the house, those are words I need to hear.) Next God promises to plant. (He has a place for those dangling, bedraggled roots!) Best of all, He promises to give His people hearts to know Him, our One true Lord. Claiming these promises, we're assured these hurting days will pass as our loving God goes to work.

Thank You for promises that give me hope for a happy future. You are my Lord, and I'm thankful. Amen.

Where to Settle

"He led them by a straight way to a city where they could settle. Let them give thanks to the Lord for his unfailing love and his wonderful deeds for mankind." –Psalm 107:7-8

As you fill box after box with earthly goods (or watch movers do this for you), do you wonder where you will settle? When we left San Diego, we didn't know where we'd be living in Kansas City. We found our apartment after we arrived. When we left Kansas City, we were heading to a parsonage with fresh wallpaper and carpeting installed just for us. Before we left the parsonage, Mike played advance scout in Watertown on a three-day search for our next home. We didn't see it as a coincidence when the home he found belonged to the former associate pastors of the church we would be attending. This couple and their daughter had just left to pursue a new educational opportunity. They needed a buyer; we needed a home. God provided for both families.

Whether we've known in advance or not, God has always led us to homes where we could settle for a time. I am thankful for His provision, and as I look back, I am thankful for unique features from each place that helped make life just a little nicer. When Justin was a baby, for instance, our apartment was located across the street from the city mall. I liked to walk there, pushing Justin in his stroller, whenever I needed a change of pace. Our first little house in Kansas City had shelves set into the walls where I could safely display treasures that otherwise might have fallen victim to our active toddler. The parsonage in Maine had a spacious porch perfect for enjoying the evening breeze.

Where will God lead you? What will He provide once you get there? Thank Him now, and thank Him then. He'll lead you along the way.

Gracious Shepherd, You've led me to many places where I've settled for a time. I have precious memories from each. Thank You now for memories to come. Lead on, my Lord! Amen.

A Good Land

"For the Lord your God is bringing you into a good land—a land with brooks, streams, and deep springs gushing out into the valleys and hills."–Deuteronomy 8:7

Genesis 1:31 tells us that after God created the world, "God saw all that he had made, and it was very good." In fact, I would venture to say that it was perfect—until sin entered the world. But that's another thought. What matters today is our knowing that God's created world is good.

You see, once we know this—that God's created world is good, then we are assured that the promise of Deuteronomy 8:7 is as true for us today as it was for the Israelites back in Bible times. Believe this now: the land the Lord your God is bringing you into is *good*. Once you get there, it may not seem perfect. You'll have cultural adjustments to make and inconveniences to accept. But if you believe in advance that your new home is good

—because God made it *and*

—because God led you to it,

then you'll have a happy future to anticipate as you pack.

Further, if you keep those two truths in mind once you arrive, the little troubles you encounter won't distort your picture of the whole. God made it; it's good. Be thankful. Be glad.

Creator of All, I believe in Your promises. The land You are leading me into is good. Thank You for all I'll enjoy once I'm there. I'll trust You, Lord. Amen.

Stuff

"Though your riches increase, do not set your heart on them."
–Psalm 62:10

Until our move to the Netherlands, we had always moved ourselves. I wrapped and rewrapped each fragile treasure, packing and repacking boxes until I was sure every item would travel well. The idea of moving all our possessions overseas was a bit overwhelming, though, so we gave in and nervously let the professionals handle that move.

About this time, I talked with a fellow military wife who told me about a time when the movers lost *all* of her family's belongings. "We were really disappointed," she said, "but looking on the bright side, we got all new stuff!" I admired her attitude, but hoped I wouldn't have to look on the bright side after my move—I wanted to *keep* all my stuff.

Thankfully, I talked with another veteran mover. This friend had moved to and from Europe twice, and most of her possessions had come through the experience well.

She told me this: "Before every move, I pray and commit my belongings to the Lord. If He wants me to have them, they will arrive at our new home. If they are lost, I trust that God has something else in mind. When the movers come, I put everything in God's hands."

Lord, help me to remember that things are just things. Everything I have is a gift from you yet still belongs to You. Do with "my stuff" what You will, Lord. Amen.

Hold Baggage

"For we brought nothing into the world, and we can take nothing out of it." –1 Timothy 6:7

Preparing for an overseas move has a way of putting the value of possessions into perspective. We learned much about this when we moved to the Netherlands.

Before the movers came, we divided all of our belongings into three groups. Group one held anything we felt we could do without for three years to be put into storage until our return. After living in Europe for a few years, we actually forgot what some of those items were and wondered if we'd ever need them again. On the other hand, we missed some items terribly and even had to replace a few.

Group two held the bulk of our property. This was crated up and loaded on a boat for slow travel over the sea. After two months in limbo between homes, we were very happy to see these belongings settled and functioning well in our new home.

The final group was the most challenging to choose. This was our hold baggage. Items in this group were shipped by air, so that we'd have them right away; in other words, these were our perceived necessities. The weight limit was small, so we had to pick carefully. Only the most essential stuff could come. Once we got to the other side, we learned that some items weren't needed after all, while some things left in other groups were sorely missed. (My iron would've been nice! And maybe a few board games for passing the time in a hotel.) Next time we move overseas, we'll be wiser as we group our belongings.

I find it amazing to realize, though, that when we leave for Heaven, everything will go in group one, and we'll never return to take it out of storage. God will provide all we need, just as He always does! Knowing this, I can happily use the resources He gives me here to build

33

His kingdom there. The value of all I own is determined by its potential to further God's work.

Lord, here or there, it all belongs to You. Help me to be faithful with all that You provide for me. Amen.

Grace and Compassion

"The Lord is gracious and righteous; our God is full of compassion." –Psalm 116:5

"Do you really want to keep this old box of letters, Janet?" asked Mike. We'd underestimated the size truck we'd need for our move from Maine to New York and were having to stuff the last of our things into every creatively manufactured inch of space. Feeling the pressure, I scolded myself for being overly sentimental and told Mike to toss the box. I still grieve over the loss.

Contained in that box were the birthday cards my great-grandmother sent when I was a child, along with her notes of encouragement and affirmation. Nana made me feel like the most important person in her life; she loved everyone that way. The box also held the card my father sent on my 21st birthday along with his memories of the day I was born. He'd wanted a boy, but God prepared his heart for me. A letter from a friend telling of her conversion and thanking me for my role in it was in the box, too. "We're sisters now!" she'd joyfully proclaimed.

Every move involves loss, whether careless or essential. God is gracious and compassionate, though. When I think of the box of letters so thoughtlessly tossed away, God reminds me that He's given me a strong memory. The most important words and pictures are ingrained on my mind; I can see them whenever I want that way.

He also reminds me that people are more important than paper. I treasure relationships with family and friends, knowing I can't accidentally throw them away! And God assures me I'll see Nana in Heaven someday. Whatever the loss along the way, God graciously provides what we need in its place. It's great to have an understanding Lord.

Compassionate Father, thank You for comfort in times of loss and for the gracious way You fill any holes in my heart. Amen.

What Are You Asking For?

"Jesus answered, 'Everyone who drinks this water will be thirsty again, but whoever drinks the water I give them will never thirst. Indeed, the water I give them will become in them a spring of water welling up to eternal life.'" –John 4:13-14

The woman wanted water. More than that, she wanted living water—a permanent source of water within, so she'd never be thirsty again. So she'd never have to draw water from the well again. So she could hide in her house and avoid the open stares and whispered comments reserved for women with questionable reputations. She wanted an earthly solution to an earthly problem. But Jesus offered the gift of eternal life that would eventually leave the things of Earth long forgotten in her past.

Are we as short-sighted as the woman at the well? What do we ask for as we face a first move ever or a tenth move in as many years?

Stability?

Security?

Friends who know us—whom we've had time to get to know?

Close proximity to relatives?

A house to fix the way we like and enjoy for the rest of our lives?

Jesus offers so much more! Ask Him for living water; then begin to enjoy your eternal life. As you worship Him daily, He'll faithfully provide everything you need. A woman who leans on Jesus is a woman who's ever content.

Father, forgive me when I focus too closely on human needs. Remind me to rely on You for what's truly essential, for the needs of eternity. Amen.

Solomon's Request

"So give your servant a discerning heart to govern your people and to distinguish between right and wrong. For who is able to govern this great people of yours?" –1 Kings 3:9

What a deal! Solomon asked for wisdom and got long life and prosperity thrown in as a bonus. (See 1 Kings 3:10-14.) In my childhood days, I tried it. "Okay, Lord, I'm asking for wisdom. Where's the money?" If it were that simple, though, we'd all be wise and wealthy. I eventually realized there must have been more to Solomon's prayer than a magic formula for receiving God's blessing.

Look more closely at Solomon's prayer, and you'll see that there was. In verses 7 and 8, Solomon admits he feels incompetent to complete the task God has given him—to rule over God's chosen people. When Solomon asks for a discerning heart, he is wisely asking for the tool he most needs to do the job God has given him to do. God offered Solomon anything (verse 5)—Solomon unselfishly asked for the ability to successfully follow God's will for his life.

As frequent movers, what tools do we most need to glorify God through our lives? Personally, I need courage and an open spirit, the ability to get to know people quickly, see them through God's eyes, and love them as He does. I also need a sense of security in my unstable world, and so I ask God for these, trusting Him to provide them along with anything else I need to accomplish my given task. It seems Solomon's prayer is still being answered; his wisdom continues to show God's people the way.

Father, provide what I need to do Your will through my life. I'll trust Your judgment. Amen.

A Good Thing

"So then, those who suffer according to God's will should commit themselves to their faithful Creator and continue to do good."
–1 Peter 4:19

If it's God's will for your life, then moving is a good thing. However, as you go through the process of sorting, packing, saying good-bye, searching for a place to live, unpacking, resettling the family, and finding your way around, you may feel that you are suffering something awful. There will be times when you won't feel thankful. In fact, you may feel downright angry and frustrated! This is the time to sit down, relax, and recommit.

First, tell God what's going on and exactly how you feel about it. He won't be upset with you. In fact, He already knows the situation; He's waiting for you to bring it to Him.

Second, go back to the beginning of the whole process. When did you first learn that it was time to move? Or perhaps even further—when did you first embark on a lifestyle that required frequent moves? Or even—what led you to marry this person whose job now unexpectedly requires many moves? Remember your prayers from these crucial points in time. Remember committing your decisions to God and knowing that they were His will for you. Ask Him now to renew the sense of purpose and determination that allowed you to proceed back then.

At this point, you may wonder if you *did* take the time to seek God's will and to commit yourself to His purpose. If this is so, ask His forgiveness. Make the commitment to wait for His direction and follow Him step by step from this moment forward. You can't travel back in time, so put aside any regrets and let God work your life out in His way. He can align all paths from any position once you give Him the go ahead. He knew you would be where you are; He's ready now to lead.

Finally, remember that God is faithful. Trust Him to work wonders as you continue to do good. He has your best interests at the top of His agenda, and He's planning great things for your life.

Father, though I suffer, I'll trust You. Your desires are best. Amen.

The Disciplined Choice

"Do not be anxious about anything, but in every situation, by prayer and petition, with thanksgiving, present your requests to God."–Philippians 4:6

Not being anxious is an exercise of the will. There are just so many things to worry about during a move! Where will we live? How will we get there? Will we get there safely? Will those in charge complete all the paperwork in time to clear the family to travel together or will we have to follow Mike later—all by ourselves—all the way across the ocean and into a foreign country—or two?! I get sick to my stomach just thinking about it—and we're not even planning a move—just now.

The Bible tells us not to *be* anxious, though. So how do we accomplish this impossible task? The Bible tells us that, too. We choose to replace anxious thoughts with prayer and petition, by thanksgiving! No matter how many times during a day (or throughout the night) those mischievous, peace-stealing thoughts try to set up house in our minds, we should turn them right over to God by praying:

"Lord, I have this concern, but I've decided not to worry about it. You are bigger than this problem, so I'm giving the matter to You. Thank You for offering to take care of this for me, so I don't have to worry anymore. And thank You in advance for working everything out in the way that's best for all concerned. I love, trust, and appreciate You, Lord. Amen."

Father, You are wise and capable, and You love me! I'm so thankful I can always count on You. Amen.

The Right Time

"There is a time for everything, and a season for every activity under the heavens: . . . a time to weep and a time to laugh, a time to mourn and a time to dance." –Ecclesiastes 3:1, 4

"Father, what's wrong with me," I prayed. "I've taught this class before, and I enjoyed it then. This time I just can't get into it." I was teaching a class based on Susan Miller's book, *After the Boxes are Unpacked.* The purpose of the class was to encourage ladies who had recently moved into the area. Ironically, I was getting ready to move *out* of the area.

"What perfect timing," I thought, when asked to teach the class. I can reread the book and prepare myself in advance for all the adjustments that come with moving. I was frustrated to learn it didn't work that way. Each week I put off studying my lesson until the last possible moment. When the morning of class rolled around, I could hardly make myself get out of bed.

"Help me, Lord," I prayed. "How can I encourage them, when I'm so discouraged myself?"

Ecclesiastes 3:1-8 put the situation in perspective. The ladies in my class were "planting" and "building." I was "uprooting" and "throwing away." You can't laugh and dance when it's time to weep and mourn. I had to go through the process just like everyone else in order to successfully come out on the other side.

Just realizing this fact, however, brought comfort and started me toward the time of healing and mending. As I tore down one household, I joyfully looked forward to the day when I could build another one.

Thank you, Father, for hope of happier times. Help me to embrace each season of "activity under the heavens" as You fulfill Your purpose for my life. Amen.

Wherever He Goes

"But Ruth replied, 'Don't urge me to leave you or to turn back from you. Where you go I will go, and where you stay I will stay. Your people will be my people and your God my God. Where you die I will die, and there I will be buried. May the Lord deal with me, be it ever so severely, if anything but death separates you and me.'" –Ruth 1:16-17

This beautiful passage shows Ruth's complete devotion to her mother-in-law, devotion born no doubt of Ruth's marriage to Naomi's son and a shared experience of sudden widowhood. Ruth was determined to go with Naomi to the ends of the earth if necessary, and she even accepted Naomi's God, our one true God, as her own to prove it. Ruth knew there wasn't much hope for two women alone in Bethlehem, but she vowed to stay with Naomi no matter what came their way.

Knowing that his vocation could take them all over the world, friends of ours used this passage in their wedding vows. The bride boldly promised to follow her groom wherever he might go, and over the years, she's done just that.

Another friend married while her husband was in college, before he'd made career plans that would take her to the ends of the earth. "If I'd known he was going to join the Army and move us around every two or three years," she confided in me one day, with the subtle hint of a grin, "I'd have married him anyway." God must smile at such examples of pure love.

Lord, moving is tough whether I see it coming or not. Help me to be the devoted spouse You mean for me to be. May my actions and attitude show determined commitment to You, my Lord, and to my spouse. Amen.

True Treasure

"But store up for yourselves treasures in heaven, where moths and vermin do not destroy, and where thieves do not break in and steal. For where your treasure is, there your heart will be also."
–Matthew 6:20-21

A few years ago, my parents were getting ready to move. Having lived in the house for more than twenty years, they had quite a bit of stuff to sort. My father asked my brother and husband to help him pull things out of the attic for the family to go through together.

At first, my brother and I were thrilled to discover a collection of childhood toys my mother had saved. Dolls and doll furniture, trucks, and games galore: pleasant memories came flooding into both our minds at their sight.

Later, as we reminisced about favorite playthings, we remembered the fire that had destroyed part of our home a few years before. Some of those playthings, also stored in the attic, had been lost at that time. Perhaps Matthew could have added, "where fires don't consume," to this passage on storing treasure.

Several months later, my husband and I were sorting through our things, getting ready for another of our moves. As I set aside toys my children had outgrown, I felt badly that I couldn't save them for my children as my parents had done for my brother and I. I'm a packrat by nature, but there's a weight limit on Army moves, and even if there weren't, moving too much stuff is too much hassle. You can't always take it all.

And you can't take it to Heaven *at* all. But Jesus talks of treasure you *can* store there—even now. As you leave some perishable things behind this move, reflect on the treasure you can keep for eternity.

Keeper of My Soul, help me to know and obey You wherever I go. As I give my earthly treasures to others, show me how to store eternal treasure with You. Amen.

Keeping Words and Deeds in Sync

"See to it, brothers and sisters, that none of you has a sinful,
unbelieving heart that turns away from the living God."
–Hebrews 3:12

Saying God is sovereign is one thing; believing it is a little more difficult. Saying we trust Him is easy to do; proving that we mean it isn't quite so. If we say we know something, our actions should show it. Often, however, the things we do reveal a lack of faith. Our actions are a symptom of an unbelieving heart.

For example, I may pause to pray with a child before school, committing his day to God's care. Throughout the day, however, I'll catch myself stewing about potential problems he may face. My words say trust; my actions say not completely.

On a bigger scale, I may wholeheartedly agree with my husband that it's time to move, that the opportunity at hand is a gift from God. If I hesitate and complain throughout the process, though, my actions reveal a discrepancy between my words and faith. If I truly believe the change is God's will, I'll embrace it enthusiastically every step of the way.

When we notice these conflicts between words and deeds, it's time to ask for God's help. We must ask Him to show us what's true, choose to believe, and act on that belief from that moment on. Then we must continue to go to God for help until our words and deeds are perfectly synchronized. If we don't, our unbelieving hearts, like magnets, will eventually turn us away from God altogether. You can't reach for two opposing points on the compass at one time. You have to choose. Let God help.

Lord, I thought I believed, but I've caught myself in an act of doubt. Like the father in Mark 9:24, "I do believe; help me overcome my unbelief!" I will trust You, Lord. Amen.

Finding Meaning

"Yet when I surveyed all that my hands had done and what I had toiled to achieve, everything was meaningless, a chasing after the wind; nothing was gained under the sun." –Ecclesiastes 2:11

If you're in the mood for a great pity party, Ecclesiastes is the book for you. Over and over, the teacher reminds us that life is meaningless. Most everything we do will be forgotten or destroyed in time. What a comforting thought. It reminds me of our last days in Watertown, New York:

I was scouring the kitchen of our beautiful home when I noticed the burner covers still on the stove. I'd purchased them only a few months before, and they'd brightened up my whole kitchen. They were little things that gave me just a bit of extra joy. But they wouldn't fit the stove in my new kitchen.

"I'll leave these for the new owner," I thought. "Maybe she'll like them, too."

She didn't. The day before we left, she and her husband came for a final walk-through. She took one look at the burner covers, picked them up, and dropped them in the trash. My feelings were so hurt!

Later I didn't blame her. She wanted to make the house her own. *My* burner covers didn't belong in *her* kitchen. I'm certain she's made several other changes since I left, just as I had changed things the previous owners had done.

Burner covers are easy to forgive. But sometimes we have to leave bigger things behind. Perhaps you've invested in a ministry that has fallen by the wayside without you. Maybe a friend who was willing to go to church *with* you, stopped attending when you moved. As you enter your new life, it hurts to feel forgotten by the old.

Meaningless.

Is life meaningless? In the last two verses of his book (Ecclesiastes 12:13-14), Ecclesiastes' teacher tells us to leave it with the Lord.

Sovereign Lord, I leave the judgment of my life's meaning to You, knowing full well that without You it truly is meaningless. Amen.

Every Evil Attack

"The Lord will rescue me from every evil attack and will bring me safely to his heavenly kingdom. To him be glory for ever and ever. Amen."–2 Timothy 4:18

After many moves, it's becoming easier to stop seeing each move as an evil attack on my personal life. I've learned to look on the bright side, to eagerly embrace both the opportunity and the adventure as precious gifts from God. Most of the time. Usually. But sometimes . . . well, sometimes I just can't help seeing the disruption to my orderly little world as an attack.

Truthfully, it hurts to say good-bye to friends I may never see again this side of Heaven. It's hard to send my children off to school in a strange environment. It's disturbing to see my pictures pulled off the walls and my belongings stuffed into boxes. I'd be lying if I always put on a perfect *Pollyanna* facade. Moving involves pain, which feels like it comes from an attack.

Thankfully, I know that the Lord is working through my hurt. If it's His will that I move on, then He will do something good in me in the process. He's preparing me for Heaven, where He'll take me when He's ready to rescue me once and for all. So as I face each move, I trust that God will bring me safely through the suffering involved. I trust Him to bring my family through, too. He'll do this every single time! We can believe He will come through. May His name be glorified in the process forever and ever. So be it. Lord, make it so!

You're my true knight in shining armor, Lord. I'll rely on You! Amen.

Praying in the Next Family

"For this reason, since the day we heard about you, we have not stopped praying for you. We continually ask God to fill you with the knowledge of his will through all the wisdom and understanding that the Spirit gives." –Colossians 1:9

"We prayed for you before you came," said my new friend Nancy. "When Jill learned she was going to move, we sat right at this table—well, right at *her* table in *this* kitchen—and we prayed for the new owners. We asked that God would bring a family who would continue to use this home for His glory. We asked God to bless you, whoever you were, and give you peace."

I was overwhelmed. Not only had they prayed for us, but God had used our family as the answer to their prayers. I hoped we could live up to the expectation, but then I realized there was no expectation. God had brought us to that house. Our job was to serve and obey as always using the gifts God had provided for us.

God answered those early prayers for our family in many ways. The home became a refuge during a head-spinning tornado of an assignment. Mike was deployed often, but the boys and I were comfortable and secure. Our family received encouragement from and was privileged to serve in both our local church and the chapel on post. And God taught me lessons I never knew I needed to learn while opening doors to ministry through writing.

Imagine! God answered prayers on my family's behalf from faithful women whom we'd never even met! Now whom can we pray for whom we don't know yet?

Father, I don't know who will be living in this house after I'm gone, but You do. If they don't know You, bless them by making Yourself known and drawing them into Your kingdom where they'll find peace and contentment like never before. If they are Your servants, let them find sanctuary here as they serve You in this community in ways You've already planned. Thy will be done in their lives. Amen.

God Rebuilds

"*Now, our God, hear the prayers and petitions of your servant. For your sake, Lord, look with favor on your desolate sanctuary.*"
–Daniel 9:17

Just as Jerusalem is God's city, His "holy hill" (Daniel 9:16), you are His temple (1 Corinthians 3:16). That makes you holy, too. In fact, 1 Corinthians 3:17, uses the word *sacred* to describe you. As a Christian, your life is sacred, holy, hallowed, and consecrated to *God.*

Therefore, if your life lies in ruins, as Jerusalem, God's city, did, you can pray as Daniel did. You can read his entire prayer in Daniel 9:4-19. Please do, and pray each sentence for yourself as you read. First, though, let's focus on purpose. Take another look at Daniel 9:17.

As Daniel asks God to hear his prayers and petitions, he acknowledges that God's only reason for restoring Jerusalem is for *God's* sake. Jerusalem did not deserve His favor or forgiveness. God owed His people nothing and could have walked away. Daniel knew this, yet he also knew the world was watching. In fact, the world had been watching God's people for years. Many rejoiced to see the demolition of a once glorious kingdom and the people who claimed God as their king. By keeping His Word and restoring His city, God showed the world His majesty.

When we ask God to rebuild the ruins of our lives, we shouldn't do so because we're uncomfortable, wallowing in self-pity and wanting everything fixed. We should ask because we want to live lives that honor our worthy God. When people look at us, we want them to say, "Wow! *God* did that!" If they do so, they may turn to God with Daniel's prayer on their own lips, giving the ultimate glory to our ever-deserving Lord.

For Your sake, my God, continue to rebuild Your holy city, one desolate person at a time. Amen.

Being Ready

"You also must be ready, because the Son of Man will come at an hour when you do not expect him." –Luke 12:40

Whenever we put a house on the market, the realtor tells us to keep it especially, extra clean and ready for potential buyers to view at a moment's notice. When one realtor called from our driveway with potential buyers in his vehicle to ask if we'd leave and let them come right in, we learned just how essential it was to follow that advice.

For one of our home sales, we had a steady stream of people coming in to view our house for weeks. With that kind of traffic, it's easy to remember to keep the house company clean.

Other sales have been more of a challenge, though. As we prepared to leave New York, our boys were four, eight, and eleven. They were great little helpers, but expecting spotless perfection twenty-four/seven for weeks on end from boys that age and their parents is a bit much.

When we put the house on the market, we scoured it for viewing. Then no one came. Gradually, we let things slide from company clean to comfortable clean to clean enough for us. The idea that someone might want to look at the house began to seem unreal.

Then the phone rang. We had one hour to get everything in order. Then we felt challenged to keep it that way—for a little while . . . until time passed . . . and things began to slide again.

Going through this experience whenever we sell a house reminds me that Jesus is coming again—and soon! This is much too easy to forget. We need that sense of urgency; we must anticipate His coming every day. For just as the phone rings, the trumpet will sound. The Son of Man *will* return.

Father, please help me to live in readiness. Fill my heart with happy anticipation and give me many opportunities to share the good news of Your Son. He's coming again! I can't wait! Amen.

Questions

"If my house were not right with God, surely he would not have made with me an everlasting covenant, arranged and secured in every part; surely he would not bring to fruition my salvation and grant me my every desire." –2 Samuel 23:5

When you begin to doubt God's love and care for you, ask yourself some questions based on some of David's last words:

1. Is your house right with God? If so, you have nothing to fear. He's leading you to Heaven His way, along the path that's best for you. Trials and challenges will strengthen you for whatever lies ahead. God is using them to prepare your soul for eternity.

But what if your house isn't right with God? Ask Him for wisdom and guidance concerning this. Determine to do everything from here on out God's way, relying on His help. Pray for family members who don't yet know Him as Lord.

2. Has God made an everlasting covenant with you, arranged and secured in every part? Yes, He has—through Jesus! The question now is: Have you done your part? If you haven't already, confess your sins and turn your life over to God. He's waiting to "bring to fruition" your salvation right now!

3. Will He grant your every desire? When your desire is to please Him and obey, He'll give you everything you need to do just that. He knows your heart better than anyone else—even you! He'll grant your deepest longings in many surprising ways. He loves you! Trust Him and see.

Father, thank You for the love and care You give even as I question and doubt. Help me to trust that You are consistently working Your will in me. Amen.

Chapter 3
Saying Good-Bye

Our Understanding God

***"For God so loved the world that he gave his one and only Son,
that whoever believes in him shall not perish but have eternal life."***
–John 3:16

"When God told you to leave California, Janet, He never promised to bring you back," said my father. I had just broken the news for the third (or was it the fourth?) time that our next move would *not* be back to sunny Southern CA. It broke my heart. I wanted to go home, but more than that I didn't want to hurt the precious people I'd left behind. Separation is painful.

But I've been blessed with parents who know our family is following God's path for us at this time. God is sending us to minister to soldiers and their families all over the earth, and part of ministering to them is going through what they go through. This includes sometimes moving far from home.

I'm comforted to know God understands. After all He sent *His* only Son away from *His* heavenly home—a separation that had to hurt! And Jesus willingly came in order to go through what we go through and to teach us how to live for God. Jesus ministers to us! I'm thankful for His example to follow—even when called far from home.

Awesome Heavenly Father, forgive me when it hurts so bad I'm tempted to question Your will. Thank You for sending Your Son to endure the pain of the cross on my behalf. Help me to follow His example faithfully, looking forward to the day when we'll all be together eternally. Amen.

A Righteous Cause

"Commit your way to the Lord; trust in him and he will do this: He will make your righteous reward shine like the dawn, your vindication like the noonday sun." –Psalm 37:5-6

My husband and I are blessed with parents who support the ministry God has given us, though it has taken us far from home and, sometimes, made it difficult to visit. We realize that not all parents are like this. For example, I recently talked with a soldier whose parents had been against his decision to join the Army. They told him he'd regret the choice. This soldier respected his parents and listened to what they had to say, yet prayerfully determined that joining the Army was God's will for his life.

Parents have a powerful influence on their children. This is good; God meant for it to be that way. Further, He meant for children to respect their parents. As children grow up, however, they must go directly to God for their life's direction. Seeking advice from parents is wise, yet final decisions belong to God. Adult children whose parents won't let go may have to take a stand in order to obey their Lord.

As I continued to talk with the soldier who took such a stand, he told me how God had honored his decision. Now that he's been in the Army for a few years, his parents have seen how well-suited he is to military life. With pride, they encourage him to make the military his career.

If you are following God's path for your life, people, even parents, will see that you are where you belong, even if you are far from home. They may or may not accept the truth they didn't want to face, but they will *see* it. Regardless of how they respond, you will have the peace that comes from doing things God's way. Commit your life to the Lord. Trust Him to handle those who question His way.

Father, Satan tries so hard to keep people in bondage to one thing or another—or even to a place. Help me to faithfully follow You regardless of his attempts to block my path. Amen.

Practicing Blindness

"I will lead the blind by ways they have not known, along unfamiliar paths I will guide them; I will turn the darkness into light before them and make the rough places smooth. These are the things I will do; I will not forsake them." –Isaiah 42:16

"I don't know what I'm going to do," I confessed to some friends. "I realized last night that I can find my way around my house in the dark. I even know that there are exactly eleven steps up to the landing and eight more up to the second floor. If I forget something downstairs, I can get it without turning on a light or bumping into anything. I know this house so well, but once we move I'll be lost!"

My friends laughed. Then one teased, "I've heard that people who count steps in the dark are practicing to be blind."

I don't know if I practice to be blind or if my mind just counts the steps to pass the time. But I do know I feel blind in the dark all over again every time we move.

I also feel blind when I think about a future in an unknown place. So many questions: Will we live there long? Will the people be friendly? Will the grocery story carry my favorite brands? Will I be able to find my way around town? Will my children be happy? What a relief to know that God goes before me. He is holding my hand and leading the way. He'll smooth out the rough spots, so I won't trip and fall. He'll never leave me to grope alone in the dark.

Father, thank You for the peace that comes with knowing Your eyes see the future mine can't. Amen.

Leaving to Follow

"And immediately they left the boat and their father and followed him." –Matthew 4:22

James and John knew that in order to follow Jesus, they would have to leave some things behind—important things! Yet when Jesus came along, they knew He was the One to follow forever, and they couldn't keep up with Jesus while carrying a boat.

Some people struggle to accept this reality. Jesus says, "It's time to grow up!" So they go away to school or get an apartment, but bring their laundry home to Mom and raid her supply closet for shampoo and soap while there. The Lord provides a spouse and children, yet these people allow their parents to dictate the way their household will be run. Jesus encourages them to accept a job opportunity in another town, so they move, but refuse to sell their house, transfer their bank account, or make new friends. A *few* of these actions may be understandable for a time in special circumstances, but on-going refusal to change once a change has taken place is unhealthy for everyone involved. When Jesus says, "Follow me," one mustn't hesitate!

James and John didn't. As soon as they heard Jesus' call, they left their occupation, transferred their loyalty from Dad to the Son, and effectively detached themselves from anything that might tempt them to turn from God's way. There was nothing left to pull them back. What a wonderful example of devotion to the Master. These headstrong Sons of Thunder submitted wholeheartedly, putting themselves completely in Christ's care. Jesus calls us to do the same.

If anything exists to keep me from following You, Lord, give me the determination to say, "Good-bye," and leave it behind. From this day forward, I submit to You alone, my Master, my Leader, my God. Amen.

A Trusting Sacrifice

"Offer the sacrifices of the righteous and trust in the Lord."
–Psalm 4:5

When one of my children was very little, he became extremely attached to his pacifiers. He never went anywhere without "ba-boo" in his mouth, and I always carried a spare or two in case one was lost or dropped somewhere inconvenient. In fact, I remember pulling over to the side of the road once on the way home to retrieve a dropped pacifier because the child wouldn't stop crying without it. From then on, I always carried a spare or two *within easy reach*.

The day came, however, when it was time to put the pacifiers away once and for all. I knew that taking the pacifiers would be a mistake. My son had to willingly give them up—to sacrifice them once and for all, to trust that he could go on without them. I didn't know how to convince him of this, though.

The solution was my mom's idea. With great ceremony, my son threw all but one of his pacifiers into the trash and waved good-bye forever. Then we explained that when the last pacifier was lost or worn out, he would bravely go on without "ba-boo" from that day on. The boy listened and eagerly agreed to the plan. Within a week, the last pacifier was gone. My son had taken his first big step toward manhood.

I cried.

My son did not.

He believed what we'd told him: growing boys don't need "ba-boos."

When the circumstances in our lives change, we can willingly offer them to God as sacrifices. We can choose to believe what He's told us: with His help, we're going to be okay. What He removes, we no longer need. What He adds, we do. Whatever happens, we can trust our

God. Moving in Him, we're moving toward maturity—just like my brave, pacifier-less son.

Father, sometimes it hurts to let go. But I'll willingly release the "ba-boos" in my life to trust in You. Amen.

Blessed Mourners

"Blessed are those who mourn, for they will be comforted."
–Matthew 5:4

I've heard several theories about what Jesus meant when he said, "Blessed are those who mourn." The most obvious is that He was referring to those who suffer loss; God will comfort them. Another idea is that Jesus meant those who recognize their sin and regret it to the point of grief; as they repent, they will be comforted. One other is that Jesus was speaking of those who experience sorrow as they turn away from worldly, yet sinful pleasures; once they've left these behind, they'll find comfort in what they left them for—a right relationship with our holy God.

I don't know which of these interpretations is correct; maybe all three are! But I do think all three can apply to those who've recently moved. When we move, we mourn the friends, family, and community we've left behind. We can turn to God for comfort as we experience this. We may also experience regret, as it suddenly becomes too late to reach out to neighbors or accomplish location-specific goals as perhaps we'd planned. If we confess these failures to God, trusting Him to help us do better in our new locale, God will comfort us in this area, too. Finally, we may find the opportunity to leave something behind that God had meant for us to give up all along. We may miss what God is asking us to turn from, but once we choose to be faithful and obedient, we'll find comfort in following Jesus.

Lord of All, thank You for comfort in times of mourning. Remind me to turn to You. Thank You for a sense of Your comforting embrace. (I look forward to the real one someday!) Help me during this move to leave all regrets and sin behind and move forward in faithful and trusting obedience to You. Amen.

For Joy

"For the joy set before him he endured the cross, scorning its shame, and sat down at the right hand of the throne of God. Consider him who endured such opposition from sinners, so that you will not grow weary and lose heart." –Hebrews 12:2-3

Consider Jesus for a moment. He left Heaven and came to Earth, setting aside His glorious divinity for humble humanity. If that weren't sacrifice enough, he "endured opposition from sinners." The statement is so matter-of-fact that we almost miss its depth. That *opposition* resulted in His death on a cross, the shameful death of a convicted criminal. I'd be screaming, "Stop! It's not fair! I didn't do anything. I'm innocent!" But Christ didn't complain. He quietly let sinful humankind lead Him to His temporary grave.

Why? Hebrews 12:2 tells us He did it for joy! How is this possible? Verse 3 says we should consider His example, so we "will not grow weary and lose heart." The example: obeying His Father gave Jesus great joy! Completing His mission on our behalf gave Jesus great joy! Triumphantly sitting at the right hand of the throne of God where we will someday join Him to glorify the Father gives Jesus joy! He endured great hardship (an understatement if ever there was one) for the sake of joy! His, God's, and our joy—all are possible because Christ obeyed.

Therefore, when moving seems as painful and terrifying as facing the cross itself (and, if you think about it, it never will seem *quite* that bad), we can remember what Jesus did for the sake of joy. In obedience to God, we can do whatever it takes for the sake of divine joy, too. Ours, Christ's, God's. Obedience to God is the price of joy—and it's worth the cost every time.

Jesus, I'll follow Your example. I'll go where You lead. I'll obey as You obeyed. Thank You for the promise of joy in Your presence someday. Amen.

Hezekiah's Lament

"Like a shepherd's tent my house has been pulled down and taken from me. Like a weaver I have rolled up my life, and he has cut me off from the loom; day and night you made an end of me."
–Isaiah 38:12

Garage sales sound like a good idea before they begin, but once the scavengers have picked through my little treasures (which weren't treasures until the scavengers begin to pick through them, of course) and taken my *extremely* valuable stuff (for practically nothing, no less), I feel as if my house has been pulled down and taken from me.

When the movers have gone, leaving only a few sleeping bags and suitcases in our otherwise-empty house, I feel as if my life has been rolled up.

And when the friend, who promised to e-mail, write, call, and forever keep in touch, remains silent month after month, I feel cut off. (Some people just don't do long distance! Trust they love you anyway.)

This is part of moving. We leave stuff behind. We pack up our household goods. We say good-bye to friends, sometimes for the rest of this life. But the good news is: this part of moving is not the end. Though the prophet told Hezekiah he was going to die, resulting in the lament of Isaiah 38:12, the Lord graciously gave him another fifteen years! (See Isaiah 38 for details.) Likewise, once we reach our new home, the Lord will give us a new life, treasures, and friends in our new place. That's why, as we go through this process, we can gratefully sing with Hezekiah, "The Lord will save me, and we will sing with stringed instruments all the days of our lives in the temple of our Lord" (Isaiah 38:20).

Thank You Lord, for hope! Amen.

Differing Childhoods

"I prayed for this child, and the Lord has granted me what I asked of him. So now I give him to the Lord." –1 Samuel 1:27-28

As we move from home to home every few years, I sometimes wonder about the impact of this on my children. I was raised in one home most of my life. In fact, I only remember one of the two moves I experienced while growing up. When I think of my childhood, I picture the house on Olive Street in Garden Grove, California where my family lived from my fourth grade year on. In fact, I still think of myself as a Californian, though I haven't lived in that state since 1989. What state will my children think of as home? Or will they be able to identify themselves with a specific place at all? Is this bad, or does it matter?

A new friend greeted me with an interesting question once: "So what states were your children born in?" My children were born in California, Kansas, and Maine. I thought we were unique until my friend asked this question; then I realized a-baby-in-every-new-state (for a while) is typical of families that move.

My children's childhood memories will be drastically different from mine. They won't be able to identify one *place* as *home*. But they will have a broader view of the world and a greater ability to relate to people from other cultures. I can't give them the childhood I enjoyed, and I don't yet know what impact moving every few years will have on them. But the Lord granted my husband and me three precious sons. We give them back to Him—and trust.

Lord, You have a different path for each person You create. I trust that the path You have chosen for our family now is preparing each of our children for his future—a life of obedience to You. Amen.

A Prayer for Sending

"Now may the God of peace, who through the blood of the eternal covenant brought back from the dead our Lord Jesus, that great Shepherd of the sheep, equip you with everything good for doing his will, and may he work in us what is pleasing to him, through Jesus Christ, to whom be glory for ever and ever. Amen."
—Hebrews 13:20-21

As you prepare to say, "Good-bye," asking loved ones to pray for you will be helpful to both you and them. Don't hesitate to invite your church family, your extended family, and your close friends to pray for God's will to be done in your life as they send you off to face a new world. Knowing those you leave behind are praying for you will give you comfort, courage, and a mission to fulfill. At the same time, praying for you will allow your friends and family to participate in your adventure as they call on God to surround you with His love.

The writer of Hebrews closed his letter with the perfect prayer for sending. He wasn't sending anyone away, of course, but he *was* saying good-bye and encouraging those he cared about to serve God faithfully where they were. Your loved ones can do the same for you.

This writer reminds us that God is a God of peace, not strife. He also reminds us that this same God raised Jesus, our Savior and Shepherd, from the dead—imagine what He can do for you! Most important of the possibilities, God will equip you with all you need to do His will. He will work what pleases Him most into your life, like a baker working just the right amount of yeast into the dough. This is possible because of Jesus and will ultimately bring all glory to Him—forever!

Great Shepherd, thank You for loved ones who ask that Thy will be done in my life wherever I go. Bless them for it as You work in them, too! Amen.

God's Longing

"Look, your house is left to you desolate." –Matthew 23:38

You stand in the middle of an empty room and look around for the last time. The walls are bare except for a stubborn nail or two left for the pictures of those who will come. The last building block has been picked up off the floor from its former hiding place behind the couch that's been boxed up and loaded in the moving van. The dust bunnies have been swept out of the corners and the floors vacuumed and mopped as they only can be when the furniture is gone. All that's left of your home is the shell of a house, truly desolate. Suddenly you feel somewhat lost. Where *do* you belong?

Matthew 23:38 paints a bleak picture, yet the verse just before is full of hope: "Jerusalem, Jerusalem, . . . I have longed to gather your children together, as a hen gathers her chicks under her wings, and you were not willing." God longs to comfort His children, and this includes you—especially at this tense moment in time. Picture the hen gathering her chicks. She offers them safety, warmth, a place to sleep, care, perhaps even love, if hens are capable of such. Jesus' words comparing His Father to a hen reveal what is available to you. And with our heavenly Father, the love is guaranteed!

There's only one possible thing keeping you from all God wants to offer at this time: you! God's children of Jerusalem who weren't willing missed out. But it's not too late for you. Like the shivering chick getting wet in the rain, run for the nest, duck under the feathers, and savor the warmth your loving Father has for you.

Divine Comforter, I seek belonging in You. Amen.

Chapter 4
Taking Off

To and For God

"Commit your actions to the Lord, and your plans will succeed." –Proverbs 16:3, NLT

The "For Sale" sign in the yard now says "Sold." You've packed boxes and tossed junk. You've given the post office your new address, but have you committed this move to the Lord?

You may be moving because you or your spouse has found a better job or because a company folded taking your career with it. You may be moving into a bigger home for a growing family or to a smaller place because your family is falling apart. You may be feeling gung-ho, ready for adventure, enthusiastic about this move, or dragged along against your will, fingernails grasping the dust along the ground. Whatever the reason, good or bad, the decision has been made. It's time to lay reasoning aside, turn face forward, and make plans for what comes next.

As you begin to do this, ask God to give you hopes and dreams to cherish and strive for (if you don't already have them). Next, prayerfully commit these to God. From this point forward, whether you have or haven't been, determine that you *will* live for your Lord. With His help, you'll be an example for others, an active member of God's family, a child of the King living up to His expectations of you. The Bible promises, if you do your part, your plans will succeed. The promise comes from God; He keeps His promises.

Father, fill my heart and my head with plans that will glorify You. With Your blessing and help, these dreams will come true. Amen.

Moving in Him

"'For in him we live and move and have our being.' As some of your own poets have said, 'We are his offspring.'" –Acts 17:28

Do you see the pun? Ouch! "For in him we . . . move" and move and move and move some more. I was so busy groaning, I almost missed the rest of the verse: "For in him we *live*." In Him, we *"have our being."* It doesn't matter how many times we move or how often we move, so long as we're moving in God.

When I was growing up, my brother and I had pet hamsters. They were cute, but so sneaky. While we slept, they spent the night devising new ways to escape from their safe and cozy cages. We started many mornings with household hamster hunts. To our great relief, we always found the furry critters. We knew they could have been lost or harmed.

After I married, my husband bought me a hamster as a gift. We reasoned that if we could raise a hamster, we might be ready to try raising kids. Responsibly, my husband bought a hamster ball to go with the hamster. When I put our pet in her ball, she could safely run all over the apartment without getting lost or hurt. What a great invention! Our hamster-raising project was a success!

When I face move after move, I have a choice: to live safely in God wherever I go or take my chances on my own. As one of His offspring, I'm content to remain in my heavenly Father's arms.

Father, thank You for inviting me to live in You. Wherever I am, You are the safest place to be. Amen.

Promotion Thoughts

"His master replied, 'Well done, good and faithful servant! You have been faithful with a few things; I will put you in charge of many things. Come and share your master's happiness!'"
–Matthew 25:21

Waiting for a promotion is one of the most stressful times in the career of a soldier. No matter how well you've done your job, there are always fewer positions available in the higher rank than in your current one. It's inevitable; some soldiers *will* be "passed over." And no matter how hard you've worked or distinguished yourself, promotion is rarely guaranteed. For this reason, long-awaited word of a promotion on the way is good news and a great relief.

Along with the good news of a promotion come new responsibilities, greater opportunities to serve, and more money. But a quick move to another post usually comes with the news, too. Though long-anticipated, this aspect of the promotion isn't always easy for the soldier or the family. It's the honor and the desired privilege that help both face the task.

Likewise, whether we're in the Army or not, we can choose to look at moving as a promotion from God. Recognizing the honor—that God considers us worthy to do something new for Him, we'll be eager to handle our new responsibilities well, ready to serve in whatever capacity presents itself (by the Spirit's leading), and happy to receive the rewards God has in store. The greatest of these is knowing that God is pleased with us; this knowledge lets us share in His happiness wherever we go.

Father, as I place my faith in You, thanks for placing Your faith in me. I remain Your servant, always. Amen.

Planning to Praise

"When you have eaten and are satisfied, praise the Lord your God for the good land he has given you." –Deuteronomy 8:10

The Book of Deuteronomy contains three sermons given by Moses to the Israelites in his last days. Knowing he could not enter the Promised Land, he was reminding them of their parents' failure, of God's faithfulness and power, and of their responsibility to obey His commands, to go where He leads. Moses wanted this generation to enter the Promised Land victoriously.

In Deuteronomy 8:10, Moses' command is pretty profound. There he tells the Israelites to anticipate this successful conquest. He says, "When . . ." Not if. And then he tells the people what to do: "Praise the Lord your God for the good land he has given you."

Moses gives the people a hope that is assured—they will eat and be satisfied. Then he tells them what to do about it. He prepares them to praise the Lord!

When we prepare to move into a new home and community, we're wise to take this approach. Even if the move was unexpected or isn't to the place where we'd hoped to go, we can anticipate good gifts from God in our new home. We can trust Him to satisfy the needs of our souls.

The same is true if we're preparing to conquer new territory by trying something new. If we're reaching for a dream or hoping to achieve a longtime goal, we can trust, if we're following God's direction and committing the outcome to Him, that the results, whatever they are, will fully satisfy our deep needs within.

Knowing this, we prepare to praise before we even march into battle. God is preparing good things for us; the praise when we receive them belongs to Him!

Father, thank You for Moses' message of hope and the reminder to praise and thank You for all things. Lead us into the Promised Land with confidence and strength. All glory is Yours! Amen.

Let God Be Your Guide

"The Lord will guide you always; he will satisfy your needs in a sun-scorched land and will strengthen your frame. You will be like a well-watered garden, like a spring whose waters never fail."
–Isaiah 58:11

When pioneers set out for the West in wagon trains, the smart ones traveled in large groups with experienced guides. Those who didn't usually found themselves alone in a "sun-scorched land," low on food and water, vulnerable to angry natives, wild animals, and unforgiving forces of nature. Even those wise ones who did travel with experienced guides often had to fight for their lives against these hazards. Those who tried to make it through on their own had little chance of reaching their goal.

As we set out for our next great unknown, it's good to know God is our Guide. Not only is He experienced and willing, He's also the Creator! He's been where we're going because He made the place. We can't find more experience than that.

Wherever we go, God wants to be our guide. If we rely on our own wisdom and resources, we may find ourselves crawling through the desert on hands and knees, drinking in nothing but dust. On the other hand, if we listen for God's voice, He'll point out the ruts in the road, direct us to shelter from storms, and faithfully lead us to those abundant springs of life.

Take the lead, Lord! I'm staying with You. Amen.

Hold Fast

***"But you are to hold fast to the Lord your God, as you have
until now."*** –Joshua 23:8

Justin was 18-months-old when we took him to the beach for the
first time. To say that he was terrified is to make light of the situation. I
grew up near the ocean, though, and wanted my son to love it as I do. I
wanted him to view God's creation with awe, not fear. So taking his
hands and talking softly, my husband and I tried to coax him to the
water. As my parents took pictures, Mike and I tried to talk Justin into
just barely touching the edge of the water with his cute, little, toddler
toes. No use. The boy wanted nothing to do with that monstrous sea.

Finally one of us, I don't remember which, picked Justin up and
carried him out to where the water was all of ankle high. Big mistake!
Justin let out an ear-piercing scream and clung with arms and legs to the
parent who held him as if for dear life. He wasn't about to risk being set
down in the midst of that swirling foam. At that point in time, the ocean
was just too big for my little boy.

Sometimes a move I'm facing seems just too big for me. I want
to scream, cry, run away, and hide. Instead, I must cling. God wants me
to hold fast, proving my faith in the Father who has always carried me
through. If He chooses to put His feet in the water, I'll trust Him to hold
me safe. I may bury my face in His shoulder as He walks out to sea. But
eventually, curiosity will drive me to peek. Perhaps God knows there's
beauty inside the monster I fear. Clinging to God, I won't miss a thing.

*Father, I'm frightened, but I'll hold fast to You. Thanks for the surprises!
Amen.*

Ignoring the Rear View Mirror

"Still another said, 'I will follow you, Lord; but first let me go back and say good-by to my family.'" –Luke 9:61

Jesus had hard words for this man who wanted to run home to say farewell to his family: "No one who puts a hand to the plow and looks back is fit for service in the kingdom of God" (Luke 9:62). If we're constantly looking over our shoulders at what we left behind, He'll have hard words for us, too.

Sometimes the home we see in the rear view mirror is full of heartbreak, challenges not quite met, or missed opportunities. If so, we might be tempted to look back on that home with regret. We may spend large amounts of time wondering what we could have done differently, rewriting our own history in our imaginations. But we can't change history. Yes, God wants us to learn from our mistakes, but we must let *Him* teach us as we move forward to accept new trials and prospects for service and growth.

Other times the home we see behind us holds happy memories and cherished friends. As we move to a new location, we may feel someone is dragging us forward by the hand as we look back with longing eyes and pouting lips. We may even feel guilty for leaving people we love. This false guilt doesn't do them or us any good. It only makes us miserable and keeps us from enjoying the place where we are.

Jesus wants us to live in the present. If we're looking in the rear view mirror as we drive away from our former home, we're not embracing the opportunities and blessings waiting for us in our home-to-be. Resist temptation. Treasure happy memories, but let go of the past. Move forward with a smile and enjoy the gift of today.

Father, I thank You for this day—for this moment. I don't want to miss this present You've given by looking back at what's past. Help me to resist that I'll be fit for Your service today. Amen.

Relying on God's Love

"And so we know and rely on the love God has for us."
–1 John 4:16

Sometimes when God tells us to do something, we act as if we believe we have to accomplish the task on our own. We pick up our trusty, though too-heavy, swords and march off to conquer the dragon alone. Sometimes we heave a great sigh as we drag our weapons along the ground. Pitifully, we look over our shoulders and mutter, "I can't believe you are sending me! Just what are you thinking Lord?"

Most likely, He's thinking, "Who said you had to do this alone?"

Believe this: the God who loves you will never send you off on your own. If He's sending you to another place, He's walking by your side. He's pointing out the scenery and the short-cuts. He's covering the dangerous potholes before you even know they're there. He's providing all you need to do His will, and He's loving you each step of the way. Rely on Him. Trust His love.

Father, sometimes when you send me, I forget You mean for us to function as a team. Lead the way, Lord. Thank You for loving me. Amen.

Being Carried

"There you saw how the Lord your God carried you, as a father carries his son, all the way you went until you reached this place."
–Deuteronomy 1:31

When our boys were toddlers, Mike had two reasons for carrying them. The first is obvious: they needed rest. Their chubby, little legs couldn't always keep up with our tall and (relatively) thin ones. Yet we never left them behind. When they tired, Mike carried them. As a family we reached our goal whether we were walking along a path in the woods or shopping at the grocery store.

The second reason was to keep them out of mischief. Once when we were shopping at the mall, Alex was riding in his stroller. We stopped to look at something in a store window then noticed the stroller was empty. We frantically looked around and caught our little monkey playfully peeking out of from under a rack of clothes inside the store. From that point on, Mike carried him. So long as he was in Mike's arms, we knew no harm would come his way.

When you need it most, let God carry you—whether you're tired or tempted. God loves you like a parent loves a child and *so much more*. He knows when life is hard for you, and He's willing to lift you into His arms. Don't resist. Relax. Enjoy the ride.

Father, thank You for arms that carry me when my feet (and my heart) hurt. Thank you for holding me tight as we pass temptation by. In Your strength we'll reach the place You have in mind. Amen.

True Strength

"For I can do everything through Christ, who gives me strength."
–**Philippians 4:13,** NLT

In science class one year, my son Justin placed three bean seeds in wet paper towels and kept the towels moist until the beans began to sprout. At that point, he planted the seeds and the sprouts began to grow. The kids who did this successfully got credit for the assignment and brought their new plants home. The teacher told these kids that if they could take the assignment one step further and actually grow beans on these plants, they'd get extra credit. Justin was determined to do this.

When the plants grew tall enough that they began to bow, Justin found some dead sticks in the yard, stuck them into the dirt beside his plants, and tied his plants to the sticks for support. That's when an amazing thing began to happen:

First, the bean plants died—all three of them. Kaput! Justin moved them to a sunnier place, gave them a bigger pot, watered them more, and watered them less. Nothing would save the little plants. To make matters worse, our new puppy got hold of the sickly sprouts and finished them off. (At least they made a meal for someone!) As all this was happening, however, one of the dead sticks began to sprout leaves. The bean plants were gone, but the *dead* stick began to thrive! (I kind of thought that should have been worth extra credit, too.)

Just as the little bit of life remaining in the stick needed soil, sunlight, and water in order to come out, our strength to do anything and everything comes from God. When we plant ourselves in His Word, immerse ourselves in His love, and bask in the light of His Spirit, He gives us the strength we need—even to transplant our lives in new communities!

Father, I thank You for the strength to thrive in each new home. Amen.

Chapter 5
Trusting En Route

People

"You are my flock, the sheep of my pasture. You are my people, and I am your God. I, the Sovereign Lord, have spoken!"
–Ezekiel 34:31, NLT

Throughout the Bible, God speaks of Himself as the Shepherd and His people as sheep. It's a beautiful analogy. Among other truths, it shows that God is watching over us all the time, that each of us is as significant to Him as every other, that we can trust God's judgment as He moves us from one pasture to another, and that He will do whatever it takes to lead us safely home—even if we've strayed from the flock under His care. I find comfort in each of these illustrations of God's character and will. I'm thankful God chose such a clear picture to help me understand His role in my life and my place in His kingdom.

Ezekiel 34:31 shows us one more important truth about God regarding this simple analogy: it *is* an analogy and God understands this. Our God knows, even better than we do, that the sheep of His pasture are *people*. Like all analogies, this one has its limits, and God understands this completely. That's important to know. This is why:

I've often heard it said that sheep are stupid, but when God compares us to sheep, He isn't putting us down. That's where the analogy ends. Sheep follow the shepherd because they are trained to do so. For them, it's not a matter of choice. God gave people free will, however. When we follow the Shepherd, it's because we choose to do so. That's why it's important for us to understand the role of the Shepherd. When we join God's flock, we submit to His will. We put ourselves under His protection and care. We go where He leads, often with no questions asked or our many asked questions unanswered. We decide to trust. We want to follow. We know God is worthy of our faithfulness. As a result, God is honored when His *people* choose to follow like sheep.

Lord, this person is thankful that You are her God. I'll follow forever. Amen.

Following My Shepherd

"The Lord is my shepherd, I lack nothing. He makes me lie down in green pastures, he leads me beside quiet waters, he refreshes my soul. He guides me along the right paths for his name's sake. Even though I walk through the darkest valley, I will fear no evil, for you are with me; your rod and your staff, they comfort me"
–Psalm 23:1-4

As I travel through life from home to home, it's comforting to picture Jesus, the Good Shepherd, leading the way. I'm a humble sheep—naive and oblivious to many of the forces around me. I'm confident in my circumstances when I keep my eyes on the Shepherd, fearful when I don't.

Because the Lord is my Shepherd, I can choose not to be in want. I may be tempted to think my life is lacking something, but I *know* in my heart that Jesus gives me everything I need. A good sheep chooses to be thankful and to trust.

I enjoy the green pastures and quiet waters. When God leads me to pleasant places, I can rest and allow Him to refresh my soul. I can serve Him happily with the abundance of resources He provides. I can worship, praise, relax, and rejoice.

Other times, He may lead me through dark valleys. This seems fearsome at first, but it's really an opportunity to grow closer to God, to allow Him to strengthen and comfort me.

Each place is different, yet as I follow my Shepherd, I know all are the right paths. He's leading me where I can make a difference "for his name's sake." He's also leading me home.

Thank You for leading the way, dear Shepherd. I'm happy to follow You. Amen.

Our Gentle Shepherd

"He tends his flock like a shepherd: He gathers the lambs in his arms and carries them close to his heart; he gently leads those that have young." –Isaiah 40:11

When my children were small, I enjoyed carrying them around. I had to give this up for one whenever I was expecting another, though. I carried my youngest much longer than his brothers, since there was no new baby to tell me it was time to let Seth walk. Because I loved carrying my children, I love the image of Jesus carrying them close to His heart, perhaps cheek to cheek in a warm embrace. He loves them even more than I do and wants to be close to them, too.

There's another comforting image in this verse, however. This one shows God's love for *me:* "He gently leads those that have young." I'm glad to know He leads me. He helped me raise my children. He continues to help us all adapt to each new home.

More important, He does this gently. He doesn't poke and prod from behind, saying, "Get your act together, Janet. You don't have time to be tired or think about yourself. Adjust your attitude. Accept your circumstance. Move on!" Instead, He patiently leads me along. If I'm tired, He shows me when and how to rest. If I'm grumpy, he encourages me to hang in there, to trust Him, and to learn something from whatever circumstance I've allowed to let me become that way. I can give my attitudes to Him for adjusting. I can tell Him how I feel about each situation. I can count on Him to help me accept or change these. He leads me gently, so we (He and I) can lead the children the same way.

Thank You, Loving Shepherd, for Your patient and gentle ways. As You carry my children close to Your heart, carry me, too! Amen.

If This, Then . . .

"When you pass through the waters, I will be with you; and when you pass through the rivers, they will not sweep over you. When you walk through the fire, you will not be burned; the flames will not set you ablaze. For I am the Lord, your God, the Holy One of Israel, your Savior." –Isaiah 43:2-3

Think back over some of the most amazing miracles of the Old Testament. God was with His people when they passed through the waters. (See Exodus 13:17-14:31.) He kept rivers from sweeping over them. (See Joshua 3.) In fact, He kept flames from setting them afire and was with them in those, too. (See Daniel 3.) If God can keep the most deadly forces of nature from doing what He created them to do, and it's obvious that He can, then we know:

When we experience a new culture, He'll be with us.

When we cross over the ocean, He'll be there, too.

When our new community seems hostile or frightening, He won't let it overwhelm us.

The Lord is our God, the Holy One—our Savior.

When fears of what's to come rattle our lives like earthquakes followed by many aftershocks, it's great to know they're less significant than the tiniest of tremors to our forever, all-powerful God.

Thank You, faithful Father, for your more-than-capable help in all situations. Amen.

Staying Close to the Guide

"A person's steps are directed by the Lord. How then can anyone understand their own way?" –**Proverbs 20:24**

Under the ground through much of the Netherlands are miles and miles of tunnels, some natural, others mined, all dark and winding. When we lived there we often took visitors to tour the tunnels under Valkenburg. These have been used through the years as escape routes for castle residents, sources of marlstone for ancient buildings and modern carvings, and hiding places for Dutch citizens and U.S. soldiers alike during World War II. There's even a chapel deep within where priests held Mass when their religion was outlawed by an invading country in a long ago time.

The tour is fascinating, but the guide makes it clear that the tunnels form a dangerous labyrinth. He tells of people who have wandered in never to come back out. I don't doubt these stories because about halfway through the tour, I always realize I'd have a hard time retracing my steps, and I surely don't know which path before me to take. To further illustrate, the guide has everyone stand still at one point on the tour while he takes the lantern and goes on without the group. Once he turns a corner, any corner, we can no longer see the person beside us or our hands before our faces. I'm always thankful when the guide returns.

Life is the same way. As we move through the years, we remember where we've been, but wonder at God's amazing methods for getting us from place to place. We may try to go back, but those who do, usually discover they've lost their way. We may stubbornly try to stand still, but the light quickly fades into oblivion leaving us lost in the dark. Either way, we learn the lesson: we need a Guide to take us through life's maze. When we finally choose to move forward, humbly asking God to lead the way, we're wise to stay close to His side. He's the only One who knows the terrain. He's the One who will show us the way.

Lord, forgive me for questioning Your direction. You know the path, so I'll follow. Amen.

A Lesson from Daniel

"Now when Daniel learned that the decree had been published, he went home to his upstairs room where the windows opened toward Jerusalem. Three times a day he got down on his knees and prayed, giving thanks to his God, just as he had done before."
–Daniel 6:10

If you know the story of Daniel well, you know that Daniel's decision to pray to God in spite of the king's decree is what got him thrown into the lion's den. (Read Daniel 6 if the story is unfamiliar.) You also know that God delivered Daniel from the lions and taught the king a powerful lesson about who was really in charge in Babylon. (It wasn't King Darius.) People often praise Daniel's decision. He chose to do right, knowing it could cost his life.

There's another lesson we can learn from Daniel, though. Verse 10 says Daniel gave thanks to God every day—three times a day. This would not be unusual for someone who trusts in God, but Daniel's situation made his prayers extraordinary.

You see Daniel was a captive, an Israelite taken forcefully from his home. (See Daniel 1.) Because he was healthy, strong, and wise, Daniel worked for the king and enjoyed many privileges, but he still lived in Babylon against his will. Further, other employees of the king were jealous of Daniel and conspired to end his life. Under those circumstances, one would expect Daniel to beg for deliverance rather than offer thanks. Yet Daniel gave thanks to God.

At some point in your move, if it hasn't happened already, you are probably going to be frustrated and wish you weren't going through what you are going through. When you reach this point, remember

Daniel. Knowing that God was in control, Daniel gave thanks. Show trust as Daniel did, and thank God, too.

Lord, I know You have a plan for me and that You are always in control. Thank you for my life and for circumstances that draw me closer to You. Amen.

A Lesson from My Dog

"One thing I ask of the Lord, this only do I seek: that I may dwell in the house of the Lord all the days of my life, to gaze on the beauty of the Lord and to seek him in his temple." –Psalm 27:4

Our family has a dog. I haven't mentioned him much before this because I'm not really a "dog person." Learning to appreciate Windsor has been one of the great challenges of my life. But one can't raise three boys without a dog, I've been told . . . many times. So Windsor and I are learning to get along.

One thing I do admire about Windsor, I'll admit, is his loyalty. If I'm working at the computer, he's taking a nap or chewing on a toy nearby. If I move to the piano, he moves to the rug in the hall beside it. If I'm working in the kitchen, he's lying under the table (where he won't get stepped on or tripped over). If I go downstairs, he follows there, too. He doesn't ask for much—just that I keep his water dish full and let him outside every now and then. The rest of the time, he minds his own business, close to mine. For a "cantankerous fur ball," he's a pretty good dog.

I can learn a lesson from Windsor. It shouldn't matter much to me where God leads or what He wants me to do once we get there. All that matters is that I'm close to Him. I want to hear Him breathe as I go about His business. I want to sense His smile when I seek assurance that He's there. I want to dwell where He is, and God is everywhere!

Master, lead me wherever. Just please don't leave me alone. To be where You are is enough. Amen.

Keeping Track of Sparrows

"Are not two sparrows sold for a penny? Yet not one of them will fall to the ground outside your Father's care." –Matthew 10:29

Come Spring in Holland, the birds would start singing very early—5:30 am! Big birds, little birds, colorful birds, fat birds—really fat birds! I'm sure there were sparrows among them. They kept up their singing until late into the evening, and though we enjoyed it, sometimes we would cover our heads with our pillows and beg the silly creatures to let us sleep—for just a *little* while at least.

Come Winter, however, the birds flew away. I always missed them, along with green leaves on the trees, flowers in the yard, and sunshine in the sky. I wonder where Dutch birds go in winter months? Italy? Greece? Mediterranean beaches?

I couldn't keep track of the birds. In fact, I couldn't be sure that I saw the same birds every day through spring and summer months. For all I knew, they were playing musical houses or neighborhoods and traveling around for fun like tourists seeing the sites.

God knows where the birds went, though. (Maybe *that's* why they sang so much.) According to Jesus, God keeps track of the little birds. And, according to Jesus, you are worth more than birds are to God. In Matthew 10:31, Jesus said, "So don't be afraid; you are worth more than many sparrows."

So when you are afraid of being lost like luggage in the chaos of a move, remember Jesus' words. God loves you, and He's keeping track. He always knows where you are.

Heavenly Father, sometimes I feel as insignificant as a little bird. It's good to know I count to You. Thank You for Your love. Amen.

Nothing Feared Can Stand

"'Do not be afraid of them,' the Lord said to Joshua, 'for I have given you victory over them. Not a single one of them will be able to stand up to you.'" —Joshua 10:8, NLT

Whether we're moving or facing a deployment or raising a child or sending that child off to college or traveling across town or the country or to another country or going to the doctor or the grocery store or doing just about anything, we can usually make a list of big and little things to fear.

But, of the things on our lists, our Lord firmly says, "Do not be afraid of them." To Joshua, He was referring to the enemies the Israelites would face as they entered and took possession of the Promised Land. To us, He refers to whatever is on our list of fears. Whatever, as in anything, as in everything we might fear!

When we choose to trust God, He gives us victory.

And did you notice? Pay attention. This is cool! The Lord said to Joshua, "I *have given* you victory." [Emphasis mine.] Joshua's triumph was assured before his battle even began!

God can do the same for us. With Him in charge, nothing we fear can stand.

Thank You, Lord! Strengthen our hearts. Please remove all fear. You are always victorious—we choose Your side and protection for Your glory. Amen.

Desiring God

"Whom have I in heaven but you? And earth has nothing I desire besides you."–Psalm 73:25

This may come as a surprise to you, but Earth isn't perfect. If you expect it to be perfect, you will be disappointed. Earth used to be perfect, but humankind allowed sin to enter and corrupt beyond repair. Since then, God has been preparing a new home for His children—and His children for their new home.

This means that if you are God's child, Earth is no longer your home. Earth is a temporary place where you will reside until God decides to take you home. He has a plan. His timing is perfect. Your job is to let Him work in and through you until your joyful homecoming day.

One cold December, I traveled from sunny California to frigid Maine with my two-month-old son. Our plane, along with most planes traveling that day, was delayed, rerouted, and even stopped for a time due to intense winter storms that stretched from the Midwest to the east coast. An eight-hour flight stretched to eighteen, and in the midst of it, I began to think I'd never again see anything but the inside of that plane. As my arms begin to hurt from holding a baby who seemed to grow heavier by the moment and my legs began to cramp from sitting much too long, all I wanted to see was my husband's face welcoming me home. The thought of his smile gave me hope, and home, once I got there, never seemed so sweet.

God wants you to look forward to meeting Him. He wants you to see Heaven as your home. For this reason, Earth's inevitable struggles are a blessing in disguise. They remind us to dwell on God. Earth's frustrations are temporary; so look beyond them as you can. Desire God and your place on Earth won't matter in quite the same way.

Father, thank You for the perfect home You are now preparing for me. Earth has nothing that compares with knowing You. Amen.

Misplaced Tears

"As he approached Jerusalem and saw the city, he wept over it."
–Luke 19:41

When our family moved from Kansas City to Maine, it was sight-unseen. The only glimpse we'd gotten of our new home was a video made by thoughtful new parishioners. The tape showed rolling hills, forestland, lakes, a pretty little church, and lots of smiling people. I was eager to see it in person, but we had to get there first.

The move took six days. Mike drove the moving truck with one of our children by his side. I drove our van with the other child by mine. Each day we traded children just for fun. The drive was interesting, but by the end of the sixth day, we were all exhausted. Then we got lost. When we finally approached Livermore Falls, Maine, it was through the not-so-lovely, industrial part of town. Not seeing any greenery or neatly manicured buildings, I felt misled and betrayed. Tears came as I shared my frustrations with God:

"We came here because You want us here, but what I see doesn't match what I saw. I can't live in this place!"

God quickly assured me that I could live in that place, and that if I'd hang in there, everything would be all right. I simply had to trust Him, in spite of that disappointing first impression.

Of course, God was right. We found the pretty church, the smiling faces, the lakes, and the forestland. All was as the people said it would be. My tears were premature.

As I approached my new home, my tears came because my imagination tried to forecast the future based on a faulty first glance. Jesus' tears over Jerusalem came because He knew the future of that place regardless of what lay before His eyes. Jesus saw sin, rejection, punishment, and destruction. He saw the truth, and it made Him cry.

Father, before my tears take over, help me to see the truth through Your eyes. And when I can't see it all, remind me to entrust the future to You. Knowing You know is all the assurance I need. Thank You, Lord. Amen.

Immeasurably More

"Now to him who is able to do immeasurably more than all we ask or imagine, according to his power that is at work within us, to him be glory in the church and in Christ Jesus throughout all generations, for ever and ever! Amen." –Ephesians 3:20-21

Through all that Alex could remember of his nine years, he had been sharing a room with either an older or a younger brother—the curse of being in the middle, you might say. He'd had enough. If we were moving, he wanted his own room.

But we were moving to the Netherlands where, we were warned, houses and yards are small. We decided we'd better prepare Alex for the worst.

He wasn't discouraged by the news, however. Instead, he started dreaming of all the things he wanted in a new house. "Not only should everyone have their own bedroom, but the house should have a *big* yard. It should be on a quiet street where kids can ride their bikes without worrying about cars." Pretty soon we all joined in the game: our dream house would include an office, a fireplace, and a swimming pool, too.

I didn't really expect to find all of that in our new home, but I did pray that Alex would have his own bedroom, the big yard, and the quiet street. Those things were important this time—but still they seemed too much to hope for.

Imagine my surprise when the first home we looked at had everything we'd dreamed of—except the swimming pool. But the bonus playroom and reading corner more than made up for that, especially in the windy, rainy Netherlands where a pool would have been more trouble than fun anyway! God's wisdom beat our imaginations again— why did that surprise me?

God, Your power to provide amazes me. More than all we ask or imagine, You provide all we need—and more! Future homes may not be so grand, but we'll trust You to know what's best for this family and Your ability to provide. Thank You, Lord! Amen.

Chapter 6
Moving In

Formless and Empty

"Now the earth was formless and empty, darkness was over the surface of the deep, and the Spirit of God was hovering over the waters." –Genesis 1:2

Can you picture it? Of course not! There's nothing to picture. The earth is formless and empty. There's only darkness to see, but God's Spirit is hovering over the waters. He's ready to create! From *nothing*, God created *everything, ev-er-y-thing,* abso*lute*ly everything.

Now picture your life. You've left it all. You live in a new place. You have no commitments, except to your family—commitments to them move with you. You don't have favorite people or places to visit. You haven't found the supermarket with the best prices or the hairdresser who will remember your name and unique style. Your house is waiting to be decorated—the way you want it, not necessarily the way you've always decorated it before. You are starting from scratch. From *nothing*.

So give it to God. This is the time. Let Him be your Friend while you're waiting to make friends, and let Him help you choose the right friends for this time of your life. Let Him show you what to commit to and what to avoid, what you have time for and what would be too much. Take Him with you to the supermarket and the hairdresser; let Him give your life the perfect makeover. Include Him in your dreams for your house.

If God created everything from nothing, and we know He did, then He can surely do wonders with our lives. Trust Him. Then watch. Anticipate the beauty He'll bring from the darkness. He loves you, so it will be good.

Master Creator, thank You for spending time on me. It doesn't seem You have much to work with right now, but I give it all to You. Make what You will with my life. Amen.

Invite Jesus In!

"Here I am! I stand at the door and knock. If anyone hears my voice and opens the door, I will come in and eat with that person, and they with me." –Revelation 3:20

Revelation 3:20 makes it clear that Jesus wants to come into our lives. He wants to spend time with us. He wants us to get to know Him. That's why He created us, after all—for fellowship with Him.

He won't force His way inside, though. Instead, He stands outside, knocking and waiting for us to let Him in. If you haven't invited Him into your life, it's easy to do. Open the door by telling Him you're sorry for living life your way instead of His. Invite Him in and let Him be Lord of your life. As you get to know Him by reading your Bible, praying, and attending church, you'll discover the best friend you'll ever have—One who moves with you wherever you go, even through eternity!

If Jesus is already Lord of your life, don't forget to invite Him into your new home. Ask Him to guide you through each aspect of your move. He'll comfort, advise, encourage, teach, and love you through it all. Talk to Him while you're packing and unpacking, decorating and learning your way around. Listen for His voice in everything you do. Trust Him as Lord of your soul and of your new home, too.

Lord, forgive me when I forget You're there. Come into my life. Come into my home. Be the Master of my house and my very best Friend. Amen.

What to Wear

"Therefore, as God's chosen people, holy and dearly loved, clothe yourselves with compassion, kindness, humility, gentleness and patience." –Colossians 3:12

After two and a half months of living out of a suitcase, I was very excited to open the boxes of clothes that I hadn't carried with me on the trip. It was like discovering a whole new wardrobe! Expanded choices of what to wear! I had packed all my favorites in suitcases to carry along. Now I was ready to put them away in favor of something else.

Did you know God has given us each a complete wardrobe that we only have to choose to wear (and never have to pack away)? Colossians 3:12 tells us to clothe ourselves with compassion, kindness, humility, gentleness, and patience. Yet how to do this is often a mystery. Most people *want* to be compassionate, kind, humble, gentle, and patient. We pray for these character traits and wait for God to unload them in our hearts—like waiting for the movers to bring those boxes of packed up clothes. But maybe it isn't a matter of delivery. Maybe it's a matter of simply putting them on.

God loves you. You are His dear and holy child. Doesn't it make sense that He would provide the clothes you need? Stop asking for what's already there. Open your closet and put on those heavenly clothes.

Father, help me to choose from Your wardrobe each morning. What joy to be clothed as Your child! Amen.

Something New

"Forget the former things; do not dwell on the past. See, I am doing a new thing! Now it springs up; do you not perceive it? I am making a way in the wilderness and streams in the wasteland."
—Isaiah 43:18-19

Not all moves are simple relocations. Some involve the tragic break up of a marriage. Some mean moving to smaller quarters or a less pleasant neighborhood because of the loss of a job. Some families move in order to get their children out of dangerous or difficult school situations. Some people move in order to escape a damaged reputation or unhealthy community. Moving can be complicated, both physically and emotionally. Every move, however, is an opportunity to leave the past behind, good or bad, and make a fresh start.

At the time of Isaiah, Israel had forsaken God. The prophet warned this people that their unfaithfulness would result in captivity and suffering. God planned to turn them over to their enemies as punishment for their sin. The punishment would not be unending, however. Isaiah assured the people that one day God would redeem and restore the nation of Israel. As the people faced the consequences of their actions, they were to forget the former things and watch for God to act, creating something fruitful in the desert.

Though moving to a new community is far from being punishment for sin, it is still a perfect time to forget the past and look to the future with hope. As we go through the process of packing and unpacking, finding our way around and making friends, we should focus on God and watch for something new.

Creator God, I'm watching. I'm hoping. I'm expecting something new and good. Amen.

What's Left?

"Because of the Lord's great love we are not consumed, for his compassions never fail. They are new every morning; great is your faithfulness." –Lamentations 3:22-23

Moving always involves leaving something behind. Our last move meant leaving behind some of the furniture that we purchased for our first home together as a married couple. Wearing out, it needed to be replaced, but the sentimental loss hurt a little. Leaving our country behind to move overseas, on the other hand, hurt a lot! We never imagined how much of our identity was tied up in our "one nation, under God." More challenging than that was our first move as a married couple. This move required leaving family and life-long friends for the first time, striking out on our own to follow God's unknown course for us.

A friend of mine faced leaving "a child behind at every move" for three moves in a row, as her "babies" started college, one by one. For another friend, moving meant leaving her marriage behind against her will. Possessions, people, places—moving separates you from some of the things you love, perhaps some of the things you see as a part of yourself.

Lamentations 3:22-23 assures us that *all* is not lost, though, and it never will be. Our compassionate God is faithful. Because of His great love, we will *not* be consumed. There will always be something left for God to work with as He molds you into the person He wants you to be.

As you look around your new surroundings, ask yourself, "What's left?" Then turn it over to God. Receive His love and compassion. Let Him create something new in you.

Father, sometimes I long for what's lost, but You understand my hurt and You care. I'll turn to You every morning to receive what You offer to me. Together we'll make a new start. Thank You for Your comfort and enduring love. Amen.

The House That God Built

"Unless the Lord builds the house, the builders labor in vain. Unless the Lord watches over the city, the guards stand watch in vain." –Psalm 127:1

King Solomon shows us clearly the difference between the house that God built and the one we labor to build in vain.

Are you building alone? Solomon wrote these words for you: "So I hated life, because the work that is done under the sun was grievous to me. All of it is meaningless, a chasing after the wind" (Ecclesiastes 2:17). Seriously, only God can give meaning to a move, value to a home, and purpose to your life. Ask Him for direction, and then follow His plans.

Have you done this? Then Solomon has lessons for you, too: "The temple I am going to build will be great, because our God is greater than all other gods. But who is able to build a temple for him, since the heavens, even the highest heavens, cannot contain him? Who then am I to build a temple for him, except as a place to burn sacrifices before him?" (2 Chronicles 2:5-6).

Solomon recognized his limitations, yet knew that building the Temple was his assignment from God. He used the most exquisite materials and hired the best of the best to do the work. As a result, while his heart remained in the right place, "The Lord highly exalted Solomon in the sight of all Israel and bestowed on him royal splendor such as no king over Israel ever had before" (1 Chronicles 29:25). Because God commissioned the work, Solomon's labor was not in vain.

Master Developer, Architect, and Foreman: I leave the location, design, and task to You. Build my house as You know is best. Amen.

Other Aware

"Be completely humble and gentle; be patient, bearing with one another in love."—Ephesians 4:2

As you settle into your new home, each member of the family may be focused on a different personal task. One or more will be concerned about learning new jobs and procedures at work. Another will want to put the house in order as quickly as possible in order to rid the home of all evidence of the move and to get on with a new, stable-looking life. Children will be seeking friends in the neighborhood. Teenagers will struggle with the politics of peers and a torrent of new teachers.

Because each of you is going in a different direction, this is a good time to ask God to enhance the other awareness in your life. Take time to sit down as a family a few times a week—perhaps every night—and listen to each member in turn. Encourage and cheer one another on. You won't be able to do the work for each other, but hearing and empathizing helps. With a spirit of humility, put your struggles aside for a time to bear with those of another. You'll all be stronger for the effort, carrying all the burdens as one.

Lord, when I'm consumed with pressing projects of my own, transfer my attention to the precious others in my life. Humble my spirit that I may hear and help. Amen.

Slip Away with Jesus

"The apostles gathered around Jesus and reported to him all they had done and taught. Then, because so many people were coming and going that they did not even have a chance to eat, he said to them, 'Come with me by yourselves to a quiet place and get some rest.'" –Mark 6:30-31

Are you tired? Is your whole family tired? Have you reached the point where you feel opening even one more box will steal your sanity forever away? If so, listen to Jesus' advice. Slip away with him by yourselves to a quiet place. The boxes will wait. You've probably already unpacked everything you *need*. Now you're down to photo albums, the good dishes you use once or twice a year, and that history paper from eleventh grade that you can't bear to part with because you worked so hard to get that *A*.

Now don't cheat and go to the local mall. Jesus is there, but He'll be harder to find. Instead, hop on your bikes and ride until you find a sunny playground. Have a picnic. Visit a zoo! Even a quiet museum is okay. Go where you can stand in awe of God's creation, where you can reflect on the works of His hands, where you can forget *your* work for a while and enjoy the wonder of His. Before you head home, take a few moments for family worship and prayer. The work will wait, and you'll be happier to do it after your time away with Jesus. Go quickly now—you need this. Slip away!

Jesus, I'm so thankful for restful time with You— and my family—among the quiet miracles of Your creation that we find wherever we go. Amen.

Wallpaper

"He has made everything beautiful in its time. He has also set eternity in the human heart; yet no one can fathom what God has done from beginning to end." –Ecclesiastes 3:11

Seth was two-years-old when we moved to our house in Upstate New York. This age made him the logical candidate for the freshly applied (by the previous owners) *Precious Moments* wallpaper in the middle bedroom. The older boys would have died of humiliation before living in *there*. We moved our precious Seth into his precious room and assumed he was settled for the next three years.

Then naptime came. Evidently Seth couldn't sleep. He grabbed hold of a loose corner of wallpaper and pulled a full sheet from bottom to top right off the wall. Fun! Would other sheets come off so easily? Sure, enough. They did. What a disaster!

Rather than try to repair the damage, we decided to finish stripping the walls and paint them a nice, boyish, shade of blue. Were we in for a surprise! As we stripped each layer of wallpaper, we found another waiting underneath. Each newly discovered layer was a little bit harder to remove than the one before. Months later (*really*), when we finally got to the bare walls, they were made of old house concrete instead of new house dry wall—and they were littered with badly patched cracks.

Once we recovered from this shock, we sanded down walls, carefully applied oodles of putty and miles of tape, and finally painted Seth's room as originally planned. If we'd known what we were getting ourselves into when we'd started, we'd have glued the *Precious Moments* paper back to the wall instead.

God works in our lives, as we worked in Seth's room. He isn't surprised by the layers of wallpaper and cracks underneath, though. He sees what's hidden—even from *our* eyes, and He's determined to do the job right. As He goes to work, we become uncomfortable with the mess and impatient for Him to clean it up. So we ask Him to please just slap a little more wallpaper on. But God won't settle for that. He's making us beautiful in His time—from the inside out, fit for eternity.

Master Craftsman, help me to be patient as You do Your good work in me. You know the effort will be worth it. Help me to believe this, too. Amen.

Wise Building

"Therefore everyone who hears these words of mine and puts them into practice is like a wise man who built his house on the rock. The rain came down, the streams rose, and the winds blew and beat against that house; yet it did not fall, because it had its foundation on the rock."–Matthew 7:24-25

I used to feel so sorry for my hamsters. I'd clean their cages and set them inside on the fresh bedding. They'd immediately go to work building their nests, arranging everything just so, scurrying about, filling and emptying their pouches, scratching in the sawdust. They were little bundles of frenzied energy until everything was just so—and then it was time for me to clean their cages again. Poor critters.

I can sympathize even more now. About the time I get my house arranged and color coordinated at last, it's time to move. Furniture newly purchased to fit perfectly in one home will seem completely out of place in another. The towels won't match the new bathroom. There won't be a single wall in the new home to hold my pictures in the arrangement I so enjoyed. I find myself scurrying around, trying new arrangements, purchasing items to fill empty spaces, tossing or storing things I once loved—a bundle of frenzied energy until everything is just so.

I don't have to live this way, though. If having a perfect house is my goal, I'll never reach it. I'll live with frustration from place to place. If building a foundation on Jesus, preparing for Heaven and trusting Him to get me there, is my goal, however, I'll find stability in the midst of chaos and peace in the midst of the storm.

Father, remind me not to take my house too seriously. The walls are temporary and what I put inside won't last. But a life built on You will always be stable! When I am discouraged, help me to think of that. Amen.

A Deserving Home

"If the home is deserving, let your peace rest on it; if it is not, let your peace return to you." –**Matthew 10:13**

Peace. The very word is restful. A home with peace resting on it—that sounds comfortable to me. I picture a clean home full of happy family members enjoying each other's company as they go about their daily business. All is calm. All show respect. All are filled with God's love. What an ideal! Can such a place exist?

Scripture says, "If the home is deserving, let your peace rest on it." What kind of home *deserves* God's peace? Truthfully, no kind does—apart from Christ. Because of sin, God's peace is unattainable. We can't earn it. We'll never do anything to deserve it. Yet Jesus told his disciples to look for worthy people (verse 11) and to see if their homes deserved peace.

A worthy person is someone who has received Jesus into his or her life. A deserving home is a household of believers who serve Christ together. Jesus makes the difference. He removes the sin. He encourages us to reach out to each other with love and acceptance. He blesses our homes with undeserved peace when we invite Him (and His servants) to come in.

Occasionally, this peace may be broken as inevitable human conflicts arise, but Jesus' presence will help us to resolve them His way, to restore the harmony, order, and calm. Turn to Jesus for solutions. Make Him welcome, remember He's there, and find His peace resting on your home.

Lord, thank You for joining this household and making the difference in our lives. We appreciate Your gift of peace. Amen.

A Cheerful Heart

"All the days of the oppressed are wretched, but the cheerful heart has a continual feast." –**Proverbs 15:15**

It's all a matter of perspective. I can think of myself as oppressed—a slave to circumstances beyond my control that force me to change location every few years. Or I can feast on a greater truth, one that cheers my heart regardless of any situation. This truth is: I am a slave set free. I *used* to be oppressed by sin. I *used* to belong to this world, living under the law of sin and death. Through Jesus' blood, however, I am free! The oppressive circumstances of this world can never leave me wretched because I am God's child.

This means that I can talk with Jesus while unpacking rooms full of boxes. I can run the dishwasher and washing machine over and over again in order to put clean belongings in new-to-me cupboards in order to please my Lord. I can decorate my home in a way that will remind everyone who lives in it of the God whom they belong to while pointing visitors toward the One we all serve. I can do each task, whatever it is, cheerfully because I know this pleases my heavenly Father. In this way, my heart has a continual feast on blessings from above, even when the tasks on Earth seem unending. These won't weigh me down so long as I'm looking up.

Heavenly Father, Thank You for delivering me from an oppressive life of sin. Please fill my heart with the joy of serving and communing with You wherever I go, whatever I do. Amen.

Combating Sin's Deceitfulness

"But encourage one another daily, as long as it is called, 'Today,'
so that none of you may be hardened by sin's deceitfulness."
–Hebrews 3:13

Satan wants us to feel sorry for ourselves during a move. He wants to bring us down, discourage us, and get our minds off God. He wants to cause friction so family members will become frustrated with each other and fight. That's the last thing you need at this time.

It works like this: you wave your kids off to school and turn back into the house planning to unpack another roomful of boxes. On your way to that room, you find three pairs of dirty socks lying on the floor in the middle of the living room. You decide to pick them up—after all, how can you organize one room when another is such a mess? On your way to the hamper, you notice that your husband scattered the contents of an office supply box all over that room while looking for something for work. He left the mess—for you, you assume. This thought in your mind begins to grow, "How do they expect me to arrange our new home if I'm always picking up after them?"

That frustration grows as the day goes on. By evening, you are angry. You greet your family with a lecture and send everyone off to make things right. Instead of feeling repentant, though, your family feeds frustrations of their own: "Here I am trying to make friends and please a new teacher, and all Mom cares about are a few dirty socks!" or "The boss expects me to meet all my responsibilities while settling in. Now my wife is nagging at home." Sin has deceived you all. Your hearts are hard.

To prevent this, be patient and quick to forgive. Consider the scene from the other person's point of view. Then encourage one another to hang in there as you all make the transition, so you *all* can flourish *together* in your new home.

Father, teach us to be considerate and kind. Show us how to build each other up to meet everyone's needs without tearing anybody down. Amen.

Hiding God's Word

"How can a young person stay on the path of purity? By living according to your word . . . I have hidden your word in my heart that I might not sin against you." –Psalm 119:9, 11

Tired of unpacking? Take a Scripture break. Open the Book and read something. You have time—for now. Yes, you want to put your house in order, but five minutes of Bible reading won't set you back too much. It may even help you along.

Open the Book and read—anything! Look for God's message to you today. Something you've overlooked before may have great significance in this moment of your life. When you find it, write it on a note card and contemplate the concept while you unpack another box. Better yet, write it in a journal set aside for just this purpose. Three weeks from now when you're trying to remember that great lesson straight from God, you can look it up and reflect on it some more.

Three weeks from now, you may be busy exploring your community, meeting friends, and making commitments. Develop the Scripture break habit *before* you over-accept and decide you don't have time. You have time now; and once you discover God's Voice in His Word, you won't want to do anything anywhere without it. Live according to His Word, and God will help you choose activities meant for you. Hide His Word in your heart by memorizing verses that speak to you, and God's Spirit will talk with you all your life long.

Father, thank You for Your Word. Help me to live according to what I find inside. Amen!

God's Blessing

"Now be pleased to bless the house of your servant, that it may continue forever in your sight; for you, Sovereign Lord, have spoken, and with your blessing the house of your servant will be blessed forever." –2 Samuel 7:29

Have you asked for God's blessing on your new home? David did. Knowing that God had chosen him and his descendants to lead God's people, David asked for God's blessing on the family line.

As you wander through the rooms of your new home, you can ask for God's blessing, too. Imagine activities that will take place throughout, and pray for the people who will be involved. For example, as you enter the kitchen or dining room, pray for your family's health. Pray that conversations around the dinner table will be edifying to all. Ask for God's blessing on your marriage as you walk into your bedroom and on each of your children's lives as you walk into theirs. When you see the entertainment center, ask God to help you choose movies, television programs, and music wisely, so you'll be able to honor Him even as you relax. When you walk through the front door, ask for God's blessing on all who will enter your home through the time that you live in this place.

Take your time as you stroll through each room. Let God bring blessings to mind, then ask and thank Him for each one. Remember God loves you! Just as He wanted to bless David and David's family so they could lead a kingdom that would glorify God's name, God wants to bless you and others through you. Ask Him. He's waiting right now.

If it pleases You, O Sovereign Lord, bless me, bless my family, and bless all those who will enter my home—wherever it is! Thank You, Lord. Amen.

Decorating

"These commandments that I give you today are to be on your hearts . . . Write them on the doorframes of your houses and on your gates."–Deuteronomy 6:6, 9

Need ideas for decorating your new home? God's given a few. According to Deuteronomy 6:9, we're to write His commandments on the doorframes of our houses. Which commandments? "Love the Lord your God with all your heart and with all your soul and with all your strength" (Deuteronomy 6:5).

I don't think God expects us to literally pencil in Bible verses on the walls all around our doors, but reminders of His constant presence scattered here and there around the house can be a very positive thing. A big, old, family Bible on the coffee table will remind you to study God's Word. Bible verses in artwork help you and your family to memorize Scripture, while showing your children the lessons God has impressed on your heart. Pictures and figurines of Christ should never be worshipped, but they can remind you *to* worship your Lord anytime, all the time, every day. They also act as a testimony to guests who visit your home. This glorifies God.

I'll never forget visiting a certain new friend in her new home. The moment I walked in the door, I noticed decorations that expressed her family's devotion to God. "This home is full of Christ's love," I thought. As the visit progressed, I realized it was also filled with His peace and joy.

Father, please help me to decorate my home to reflect the love You've put in my heart, to remind myself and my family of Your presence, and to glorify Your name to guests You bring our way. Amen.

Drive On!

"Do everything without grumbling or arguing." –Philippians 2:14

There's a saying in the Army that many learn to hate: "Suck it up and drive on!" It means, "Stop whining and do what needs to be done." Move *forward*.

There are times just before or after a move, however, when I don't want to move forward. Maybe I'm tired of packing or living out of boxes. Maybe I'm lonely and missing a good friend. Maybe I just want to sit down, look back over the horizon, and whine for a little while.

This negative attitude can be dangerous. Remember the Israelites in the desert. (The book of Exodus tells their story.) When things didn't go the way they planned, they actually wanted to go back to the slavery in Egypt that they had begged God to rescue them from. (See Exodus 16:3.) As a result, they ended up eating manna in the desert for 40 years. Their story is in the Bible to teach us something significant.

God doesn't want to drag me kicking, screaming, and complaining from one place to another throughout my life. He wants to lead a willing child to the Promised Land. If I'm too busy complaining about the straw and bricks I left behind, I'll miss the milk and honey. True—sometimes I must leave something or someone precious behind. But each new location has something sweet to offer. I'm learning to look for it with anticipation and thanksgiving. When I want to stop and whine, I must drive on!

Father, please forgive my moments of ingratitude and the spirit of complaining that sometimes takes over when I move or take on a challenging new task. Help me to see your gifts in each and to accept them with a thankful heart. Amen.

The Sanctuary Spot

"Come to me, all you who are weary and burdened, and I will give you rest."–Matthew 11:28

Setting up a sanctuary spot in your new home is an easy thing to do. A table by an open window with a peaceful view could work. You may prefer a comfy chair near a shelf full of books. Some ladies like the bathtub, and some have even been known to hide in their closets. Mine is a little, blue loveseat that's been with my husband and I since the early days of our marriage. Wherever it is, is my sanctuary spot. In our last home, it sat in front of a big, picture window in a "great room" that was usually full of sunlight during the day. In our current home, it sits in an attic room under a window in the sloping roof. The small couch is my thinking place, my praying place, and my stress-free spot for working problems out.

Sometimes I go there to relax and read. Sometimes I go to meet with God. Sometimes I go to hide from my husband and children and the noise that naturally comes to a home full of boys. Sometimes I go just to sit or to think or to cry, but I always go for rest and I always find God waiting for me there on this quest. When I go in search of Him, I find everything I need.

Each time you move to a new location, find a space to call your sanctuary spot. Fill it with familiar items that make you smile—books, a magazine rack, scenic pictures that calm your soul, a rug, a throw pillow, whatever *you* like. You may need to rearrange the pieces from home to home, but their existence will still make the spot feel like your own. Then, when you first feel alone (or *want* to be alone), go to this place. Invite God to meet you there. His reassuring presence will let you know He's made your house a home.

Father, I know You are with me always wherever I go, but thank You for meeting me in my sanctuary spot. Thank You for rest in the midst of chaos. Thank You for putting peace in my soul. Amen.

Chapter 7
Embracing Loneliness

No Pillow

"Jesus replied, 'Foxes have dens and birds have nests, but the Son of Man has no place to lay his head.'" –Matthew 8:20

Matthew 8:18-22 records a discussion between Jesus and two men who thought they were ready to follow Jesus. When the first declared his willingness to follow Jesus wherever He would go, Jesus made it clear that He had no earthly home.

Sometimes I feel that I have no earthly home either. If I suffer a few defeating days in a new location, I'll begin to think to myself: "I just want to go home," and I wonder if closing my eyes and clicking my heels together three times will get me there. That's when I realize I don't know where there is.

A few years ago, I visited my family in California. My mother introduced me to her friends at church as "my daughter from New York." A few weeks later, I was talking with a new friend in New York. She asked me where I came from. I answered: "I'm from California." In our next location, I told people I'd come there from New York, but on my next visit "home," Mom introduced me as her daughter from the Netherlands. Sometimes it seems wherever I am, home is someplace else.

Jesus had no place to lay His head, but He had a clear purpose—to show people like us the way to our true home. It's not time to go there yet, so for now I'm thankful I at least have a pillow on a bed in a home *somewhere*. So far that's always been true. I'm also thankful that Jesus understands how I feel when I feel that I just don't belong. Did He ever feel He *belonged* here on Earth? I don't know. But Jesus had a job to do, and that was His focus.

Lord, please make that my focus, too. With You, I'm home. Amen.

Ice Storm Isolation

"And the peace of God, which transcends all understanding, will guard your hearts and your minds in Christ Jesus."
–Philippians 4:7

No e-mail. No phone. No electricity. No television. We'd been living in our new home for a week when the "storm of the century" took it all out. For the first time since we'd begun our travels around the United States, I couldn't call my parents—and I desperately wanted to! Our boxes weren't even unpacked. To make things worse, my husband's unit was scheduled to leave for a month-long training exercise in Panama. There's no ice in Panama! Suddenly, I was facing no husband, no parents, no friends, and no sense of home. My isolation seemed complete, and panic was setting in fast.

But God was there. He's always on-line. His phone lines can't be cut. We can always reach Him in a crunch—and with no e-mail, no phone, no electricity, and no television, I really had nothing better to do than read my Bible and pray. In fact, I quickly realized that even *with* all of the gadgets, I would have had nothing better to do than spend time with my God.

A few weeks later, when all of our modern conveniences were running again, several new friends in our new church testified about how God had reached out to them through the crisis. They also told how He'd directed them to reach out to each other (and our family, too). Our community learned that when we turn off all the noise, that's when we hear God.

Father, remind me to quiet my house often, so I can quiet my heart and listen to You. Thank You for being there whenever I feel cut off. Amen.

For This Reason

"That is why a man leaves his father and mother and is united to his wife, and they become one flesh." –Genesis 2:24

Imagine for a moment, the young girl fresh out of high school who marries her childhood sweetheart. Days after the marriage, Prince Charming whisks her from the only home she's ever known to build a new home with him far away. A romantic adventure with the man of her dreams is the promise— until reality lets her down hard.

Before the boxes are even unpacked, the love-of-her-life is deployed or sent on a business trip or finds himself working two jobs in order to make ends meet. The lonely bride's first thought: "Enough of this! I want to go home!"

After several years of marriage, I still found myself longing for "home" on occasion whenever things didn't go as planned in a new place. Of course, I would imagine taking Mike and our boys with me. Then I'd realize that with them all would change. But I would never ever want to go without them, so I knew I didn't really want to go back. What I longed for was just for us all to be "home." At this point, God would gently remind me that home was right where we were.

What a comforting thought! Since I've been married, Mike's home, wherever that is, is *my* home—even when he's not there.

Father, when my thoughts turn toward the home that was, bring them back to the home that is. My new home is a gift from You. I will always be thankful for Mike. Amen.

Everlasting Love

***"The Lord appeared to us in the past, saying: 'I have loved you with an everlasting love; I have drawn you with unfailing kindness.'"* –Jeremiah 31:3**

If ever you start to feel lonely, stop what you are doing. Then find a quiet spot and reflect on God's love. Remember times when you experienced His presence in the past. Perhaps think of the day you first learned of His love; He drew you to Himself, you know, with kindness and everlasting love. Think of times of grief when God sent comfort and peace or times of triumph when you finally understood a lesson He had been trying to teach. Try to remember at least one "close encounter" from each location you've lived in. How did you feel to know that God was directly involved in that moment of your life? Take your time to fully reflect on your spiritual journey with God.

Don't stay in the past, however. The verse immediately following today's Scripture turns to the future: "I will build you up again and you . . . will be rebuilt." Just as God has loved you in the past, He loves you now. He's building again! This is true! You are not alone. Your God is at work even now creating what's best for you. As you patiently wait, soak in all you can of His endless supply of love. Then when God brings new people your way, you'll have what you need to accept them as He does and draw them to Him as He drew you.

Father, my past, present, and future belong to You. Let memories of the first help me in the second to prepare me for the third as I absorb Your everlasting love. Amen.

Taken for Granted

*"Let them give thanks to the Lord for his unfailing love and his
wonderful deeds for mankind, for he satisfies the thirsty and fills
the hungry with good things."* –Psalm 107:8-9

Shortly after the ice storm of 1998 left our community without power for eight days, the boys' school did a project based on a lesson the children learned through the experience. In each classroom, children made two lists: one of needs and one of wants. The ice storm made the difference surprisingly clear. Children learned they could live without computer games or cable TV. They survived without telephones or CD players—what they used in 1998. In fact, their list of essentials boiled down to things like air, food, water, and heat. Even electricity, something we take for granted, became a luxury item, though we were certainly happy to get it back.

It's tempting to think that we *need* a certain home in a specific location, that our children *need* a stable (location-wise) home. Truthfully, though, all we *need* is God. "He satisfies the thirsty and fills the hungry with good things." In other words, He meets our most genuine needs. Further, His love for us is unfailing and he works *wonderfully* on our behalf. We're spoiled, yet we take it for granted. God has already given us more than we'll ever deserve. We must recognize the fact that though our power, telephone line, and even our air supply can be suddenly cut-off, ultimately that won't matter if we have God's presence in our lives. We might not always be as comfortable as we'd like to be, but if we're trusting God, we have all we need.

Lord, I don't thank You nearly enough. You've given me a family and friends, a world to live in, all I need and more. Most important You gave Your Son and Your Word, so I can know You and grow to love You more. For all this and so much more, I thank You now. Amen.

Overcoming Trouble

"I have told you these things, so that in me you may have peace. In this world you will have trouble. But take heart! I have overcome the world." –John 16:33

The hardest move my husband and I ever faced was our first. As we left San Diego for Kansas City, friends assured us everything would go smoothly. "You'll never be happier than when you're doing what God wants you to do," they'd say. Then they'd tell us how brave we were to be moving halfway across the country without jobs or a pre-selected home.

We may have been brave, but we were also naïve. Apartments were hard to find, and we ended up paying more for rent than we'd anticipated. For Mike, finding a job was difficult, too. We had to sell a car to pay our rent before he found his first job there as a security guard in a mall. His small salary had to be enough until he could find something better. His attending seminary was beginning to look like the impossible dream.

One day I'd had enough. The baby had been sick. I'd been sick. Rent was coming due, and Mike had no new job in sight. I threw myself on the bed and sobbed. Then I angrily prayed, "Why did You bring us here, Lord, if You didn't plan to provide for us? You promised we'd be happy if we followed You!"

But God never promised that. He promised to guide us. He promised to be with us. He promised a future with Him in His heavenly home. He promised to give us peace in all circumstances, but He never promised they'd be perfect circumstances.

As the years have passed, I've come to realize that life is a series of obstacles to overcome. Sometimes things go smoothly, but sometimes life is hard. We all face our share of challenges. Our choice is to face them with God, or to fight our way through alone.

Jesus, You warned I'd face trouble. I choose to face it with You. Amen.

Closer Than You Think

"The Lord is near to all who call on him, to all who call on him in truth." –Psalm 145:18

When you find yourself alone in a new place with no friends, no commitments, no direction, it's easy to imagine that God is gone, too. You moved to Zimbabwe or Timbuktu or some other distant land (the Netherlands?), and God stayed in the States with your family and friends. Loneliness is a fearsome thing. But the Bible tells us that God is near to *all* who call on Him. That *promise* includes you.

So next time you feel God has left you alone, curl up in a big, warm blanket in your favorite rocking chair or a cozy corner of your couch.

Now meditate on God. What do you know about Him? How have you experienced His existence in the past?

Look around you. What evidence suggests His companionship *now?*

Finally, reflect on His love. Let His Spirit bring portions of Scripture to mind confirming His presence in your life at all times.

Once you've grasped the truth that God will *never* leave you alone, talk to Him. You'll know He's there, whether you sense Him or not, and that fact will comfort you.

Father, what joy and peace comes from knowing You are always near. Thank You for this assurance. I love you, Lord! Amen.

A Place near God's Altar

"Even the sparrow has found a home, and the swallow a nest for herself, where she may have her young—a place near your altar, Lord Almighty, my King and my God." –Psalm 84:3

Today's altars are places where people go to pray—to ask forgiveness for sin, to ask for help in especially trying times, to worship, praise, and give thanks to God. In Old Testament times, altars were places of sacrifice. The Book of Leviticus begins with a list of the kinds of offerings the Israelite people were to leave on God's altar—burnt offerings, grain offerings, fellowship offerings, sin offerings, and guilt offerings. In both cases, past and present, the altar reminds God's people of His presence. We go there to meet Him. We go to offer something— ourselves! We go to restore or build our relationship with God.

In that light, it makes perfect sense that a fragile bird (or a person who moves from place to place) would seek a home near God's altar. God is the creator of all. He understands our minds, emotions, wills, longings, and concerns. God is the sovereign ruler of the universe. He is in control of it all! God loves His people—including you and me. And God is always available—wherever we are!

When *home* seems like something lost and faraway, we can take our lives to God. In His presence, we are home. When we're concerned about finding a safe, secure environment for our young, we can take them to God, too. Once they discover His presence, they will know what it is to be home. For *home* is with God, and God is with us—forever!

Father, when I feel lost, remind me that with You in my heart, I'm always home. Amen.

A Teachable Spirit

"Take my yoke upon you and learn from me, for I am gentle and humble in heart, and you will find rest for your souls."
–Matthew 11:29

One premise of this book is that God is in control. He has a plan for each person's life. Therefore, we can blame Him for our circumstances, or we can trust Him with them. We can fight Him with a bitter heart, or we can meekly follow with joy. This is what Matthew 11:29 is all about.

When a farmer puts a yoke on a pair of calves for the first time, those calves quickly learn that if they fight and struggle, they'll get twisted and tangled until they can't even move. The process involves pain and frustration for everyone. Only the farmer can straighten out their mess and only once the calves settle down. Once they learn to work together, though, moving where the farmer wants them to go, they can enjoy a pleasant and productive walk. The farmer cares for the team; the team helps him accomplish his task.

It's the same for us. If we take Christ's yoke on our shoulders and learn from Him, we can enjoy a pleasant and productive walk through life. Serving Him will be a restful experience as we take each careful step under God's loving care. When we fight Him, however, we'll find nothing but turmoil and pain. God doesn't want this for us. He has a better plan. Determine to be teachable, and He'll show you the best way.

Father, I submit to Christ's yoke. Please teach me and give me Your promised rest. Amen.

God Is the Glue

"He is before all things, and in him all things hold together."
–Colossians 1:17

Moving is complicated enough without surprises like the one my friend received just after one of her moves. Her husband reported for duty and was immediately deployed. She was told he'd only be gone for a few days, but his time away was extended for a few months. This friend found a home, settled children into school, greeted movers, unpacked boxes, arranged furniture, opened a bank account, and discovered her new community all by herself. She didn't even know how to reach her husband for a comforting word or bit of encouragement. She was on her own.

But she wasn't completely on her own. God was there, like He always is. He knew what she'd be facing before she got there. He prepared the way and held everything together—including her marriage. By believing that God had done this for her, my friend was able to do what needed to be done without the help of her spouse, which freed him to accomplish what he needed to, knowing she'd welcome him home with open arms. In fact, she'd welcome him to their *new* home, a ready sanctuary for a soldier just returned.

Father, when the unexpected interferes, remind me to trust in You. I know You've gone before me to pave the way. You've prepared where I wasn't able. You hold it all together—You're the glue! Amen.

Choosing Hope

"So with you: Now is your time of grief, but I will see you again and you will rejoice, and no one will take away your joy."
–John 16:22

One of the greatest gifts we receive from reading the New Testament is hope. The angels offered it to the shepherds on the night Christ was born as good news that would cause great joy (Luke 2:10). Jesus offered it to His disciples in John 16 when He assured them their grief would turn to joy. Hope is one of the "three" that remain in 1 Corinthians 13:13. Paul even tells us to be joyful in hope (Romans 12:12). The whole New Testament is splattered with words and phrases meant to give us hope today!

We find hope in the Old Testament, too. Job boldly proclaimed, "Though he slay me, yet will I hope in him" (Job 13:15). David declared throughout the Psalms that his hope was in God. Clearly hope is something of value, something we should seek.

Jesus' words of John 16:22 show us why. When we grieve, and we will in this life whether we ever move again or not, hope opens the door for joy to come in and take grief's place. Jesus was going away, and the disciples felt lost. Jesus gave them hope of their reunion with Him and eternal joy. Focusing on His promise chased away grief.

When I feel as if I just don't fit in anywhere or I miss someone so much my heart fills with pain and my eyes with tears, claiming hope helps me to look beyond grief. I can look forward to reunions—even when I don't know their date. I can pray for God to bring me new friends. I can realize that life is always changing, so what's true of one day, week, or year, probably won't be true of the next. Most of all, I can talk with Jesus anytime, looking forward with hope toward the day I'll talk with Him face to face. Focusing on loss produces despair. Choosing hope brings joy.

Thank You for words of hope, dear Jesus. When I hurt, I'll look forward with joy. Amen.

The Comfort of Citizenship

*"But our citizenship is in heaven. And we eagerly await a Savior
from there, the Lord Jesus Christ, who, by the power that enables
him to bring everything under his control, will transform our lowly
bodies so that they will be like his glorious body."*
–Philippians 3:20-21

Our family moved to the Netherlands just a few months before
September 11, 2001. I didn't realize it until our plane landed in Chicago
in December of 2004, but from that tragic September day forward,
something inside of me didn't really believe that I would ever again
see home—defined here as the US of A. Overall, I enjoyed living in the
Netherlands, but I always knew my citizenship was somewhere else.
There was this tension deep inside of me, fear that I would always be
a stranger in a strange land.

When we arrived at the airport in Amsterdam for our flight
home, something inside me feared they wouldn't let me leave.

When we landed in Chicago several hours later and stood in the
customs line, something inside me feared they wouldn't let me through.

These fears were ridiculous—and I often told myself so, taking
every thought captive, again and again and again, and praying for God's
peace and protection, blessing and favor. When we finally crossed that
customs line, the agent, knowing we were a military family, actually
said, "Welcome home!" For the first time ever, I truly understood the
impulse to bow down and kiss the ground. Instead, I praised my God for
doing what I'd longed for so long, for bringing me safely home.

I'm pretty sure this is what the Apostle Paul was trying to
communicate to the Philippians in chapter 3 of that letter. The message
is true for us, too. Right now, we live as strangers in a strange land.
Sometimes we're comfortable. Sometimes we're not. But we always live
with the tension of knowing we aren't really living at home—this time

defined as Heaven. Yet, we need not fear. Our Savior has already cleared customs on our behalf. When the day comes for each of us to cross that line, it is certain we will hear the Agent say, "Welcome home!"

Father, when fears threaten to steal our joy, remind us to take every thought captive and rest in the assurance that our citizenship is in Heaven now and for all time—thanks to Jesus Christ, Your Son. Please help us serve You faithfully throughout this earthly assignment while looking forward with joy to the day when Jesus brings us home. Amen.

Chapter 8
Getting Lost

Greatly Emboldened

"When I called, you answered me; you greatly emboldened me."
–Psalm 138:3

Some people fear heights. Some people fear spiders. I fear getting lost. Whenever we move to a new community, I try to let my husband do the scouting, waiting to venture out on my own until I have a comfortable feel for the land. I'd have made a lousy pioneer.

Living in Europe where the houses were built before the roads, making the concept of a city grid non-existent, this fear was magnified. I thought I'd never be comfortable driving on that continent. One day, however, my son was invited to a youth group party at an unfamiliar house in a yet unvisited city about forty minutes away from our home. My husband wasn't available to take him, so I was tempted to say my son couldn't go. In my heart, though, I knew this wasn't right. My husband confirmed this, looking into my eyes with compassion, and saying, "I know this will be hard for you, but you have to do this for Justin's sake."

Sometimes we have to step out of our comfort zone. My son needed the opportunity to make and be with friends his age. The responsibility to get him there fell to me. And so, I prayed throughout the day, asking God to give me courage and wisdom, to protect me and to help me find my way.

When the moment of truth arrived, I was calm. I was happy to discover that my son was alert, seeing signs easily missed. We passed a few essential turns and ended up on one completely wrong street, but we were always able to backtrack without trouble and the venture was a success. On the way home, I thanked God for helping me to conquer a fear, take a bold step, and become a little more confident as He wants me to be.

Father, thank You for a wise husband, a helpful son, and Your courage: gifts from You to help me overcome a fear that hinders my service to You. Amen.

Our Strong Tower

"The name of the Lord is a fortified tower; the righteous run to it and are safe." –Proverbs 18:10

When our family lived in the Netherlands, the Valkenburg Castle was one of our favorite places to explore. Situated on the highest hill in town, this castle must have been a challenge for foes to reach. Holes in the walls allowed archers to shoot those enemy soldiers who were able to make the climb before they could enter the fortress-like structure. The walls themselves were wider than my husband is tall, making infiltration nearly impossible. One final advantage for castle dwellers was the extensive maze of underground tunnels through which they could escape. Enemies who were unfortunate enough to find the entrance from the castle into these tunnels would quickly find themselves hopelessly lost beneath the ground.

If you are feeling alone and vulnerable in your new area, don't hesitate to call on God's name. He is a strong tower of safety, and you won't even need an underground tunnel system for backup. The enemy *cannot* get through God. Resting in Him, you are safe.

Father, I thank You for the security that comes from knowing Your name. I come to You. Amen.

Sleep

"In peace I will lie down and sleep, for you alone, Lord, make me dwell in safety." –Psalm 4:8

"Who's winning over there?" asked my weary husband, "You—or the pillow?" The wrestling match had gone on for some time. I'd turn over, beat the pillow into submission, try to relax, give up, flop over, beat the pillow some more, and sigh in frustration. I was thankful Mike could see the humor in the situation; I just wanted to sleep—and to let *him* sleep.

Sometimes finding the perfect sleep spot takes me a very long time. I toss and turn until every seam is straight, every wrinkle smoothed out, and every blanket perfectly balanced. Only *then* can I relax. At least my husband has no doubts he's married a princess—a pea under my mattress would keep us both up all night!

I've learned, however, that my tossing time tends to expand in relative proportion to the stresses in my life. If I'm facing a big unknown, like an out-of-state move or a new school year for the boys or a visit to a new dentist or a first drive through town alone, I'll probably have more trouble finding that comfortable spot in my bed. This is when I need to toss my cares over the fence, one at a time—like sheep—into God's hands. Knowing He makes me to dwell in safety helps my husband sleep in peace.

Now I lay me down to sleep. I pray, O Lord, my cares You'll keep. Amen.

Waiting

"Who among you fears the Lord and obeys the word of his servant? Let the one who walks in the dark, who has no light, trust in the name of the Lord and rely on their God." –Isaiah 50:10

Even Jesus asked, "Why?" He'd followed His Father every step of the way, obeyed perfectly, and surrendered His will completely. Then the darkness came—the darkest darkness of all. As our Savior, God's Servant, hung on the cross, paying for our sins, He asked, "Why have you forsaken me?" (Matthew 27:46, Mark 15:34).

But he also declared, "Father, into your hands I commit my spirit" (Luke 23:46) and "It is finished" (John 19:30). Though Jesus felt lost and forsaken, he chose to trust His Father. He *knew* God's will would be done.

As I child, I often went camping with my family. My parents told me that if I got lost, I should stay put, so they could find me. If I ran frantically around looking for them, I would be harder to find. I might move deeper into the woods and closer to danger. My parents warned me to wait.

When we feel lost and alone in this world, forsaken and forgotten, we should follow the same advice. We can call for help through prayer. We can reach for God through the darkness, hoping to feel the reassuring grip of His hand. But we should remain calm and patiently wait for His reply instead of racing around in a panic or allowing ourselves to be overcome by anger and frustration. God knows where we are, and so we can commit our spirits to Him when all is dark, trust that His will *will* be done, and wait for His work to be finished in our lives as He has planned.

Father, I believe You will show me the light in Your time. Until then, I'll wait, pray, and trust. Amen.

Straight Ahead

"Let your eyes look straight ahead; fix your gaze directly before you." *–***Proverbs 4:25**

"I thought this move was part of God's plan, but everything has gone wrong since we moved here. Maybe this wasn't God's will after all."

Sound familiar? Doubt is one of Satan's favorite tools, and he gleefully uses the circumstances in our lives to cause it. Whenever one of God's children prayerfully commits to a move or a job or a marriage or any task that will further God's kingdom, Satan immediately throws wrenches into the works, hoping to cause doubt and indecision. Why? Because he knows that if we're looking backward, we aren't moving forward. Once we begin to question our own actions, we stop growing, we stop building, we stop maturing, we stop helping. In fact, that's when we become help*less*.

The time to question is before you commit—with God's help through prayer and Bible study. Once you make your decision, move forward with confidence, keeping your eyes fixed straight ahead. If doubts assail, don't look back. Instead, get on your knees and ask for God's reassurance and encouragement. He'll gladly give it, knowing you've learned to trust in Him. *If* a course correction is needed, He'll gladly give that, too. Just let it come from Him, not from discouraging circumstances and setbacks. Fix your gaze on God and you'll move forward all the way.

Father, some situations tempt me to look back to the place I came from. I know this is not Your will. Remind me to keep my gaze focused on You. Thank You, Lord. Amen.

Fear's Snare

"Fear of man will prove to be a snare, but whoever trusts in the Lord is kept safe." –Proverbs 29:25

If doubt is one of his favorite tools, fear must be one of Satan's favorite emotions. He'll do whatever he can to convince you to embrace it as an ally. In reality, it's a paralyzing trap.

You fear a new acquaintance's negative opinion, so you form a negative opinion of her (a defensive wall) to protect yourself.

You fear getting lost or being embarrassed, so you stay home.

You fear confrontation, so you remain silent—and suffer that way.

Fear keeps you from making new friends, discovering God's abundant wonders, or growing as you meet challenges and work to understand another person's heart. In summary, fear ties you up in knots and leaves you alone in the prison you've made for yourself.

God doesn't want this for you.

So when you feel fear creeping into your heart, resist the urge to say, "There you are! I'm glad you're here. Tell me how to handle this situation *safely*."

Instead pray, "Take this emotion away from me, Lord. Replace it with the courage that comes from trusting You. Show me how to handle this situation *wisely*, and I will obey."

Father, sometimes Fear seems to be a constant companion. I know that he's hurtful to me. Remind me to listen to Courage instead. I choose to trust in You. Amen.

Trials

"Dear friends, don't be surprised at the fiery trials you are going through, as if something strange were happening to you."
–1 Peter 4:12, NLT

As I was driving around another one of the ever-present detours in our new city, I couldn't help but reflect on some of the problems my family was facing. I still felt lost most of the time and, therefore, afraid to go to the more unfamiliar parts of town. Mike's assignment was turning out to be busier than we'd anticipated, forcing him to spend extra time in the office and less at home. The boys found the high-pressure environment of their new school to be frustrating at times; each was showing a unique sign of strain.

As I reflected on these struggles, I seemed to feel God say, "Congratulations, Janet! Your family is *normal!*" And with that simple revelation, I was able to relax.

Life is full of trials. Every person on the planet has a problem or two or ten to overcome. I was frustrated not with the problems, but because of their very existence. Expecting perfection, quirks in the plan threw me off. Once God revealed our family's normalcy, though, I was able to embrace the problems as challenges to solve and lessons to learn.

A child-development specialist friend once told me not to be too quick to solve my children's problems for them. When two-year-old Alex's ball slipped through the child safety gate just beyond his reach, she stopped me from getting it for him. Instead we watched as his little mind went to work. Looking around, he found a toy that would slip through the grid of the gate to reach the ball. He got it himself, and his self-esteem grew. Likewise, we grow as God allows life's trials to teach us. He's watching, as I watched Alex, to make sure we aren't overwhelmed. But He wants us to grow, and He's pleased when we do.

Thank You for trials, Lord. Help me to endure. Amen.

God Plans

"'For I know the plans I have for you,' declares the Lord, 'plans to prosper you and not to harm you, plans to give you hope and a future.'" –Jeremiah 29:11

When Mike and I left our college town of San Diego for seminary in Kansas City, our plans were to attend seminary together, graduate, and head for the mission field as soon as possible. Things didn't go the way we planned, however. Events in our lives forced me to put off going to seminary, and I eventually realized God didn't want me there at all. Within months of our arrival, we also began to see that God might have something other than a traditional mission field in mind for our role in His church. Confused and discouraged, we wondered why God had led us to move halfway across the country for disillusionment and shattered dreams.

We could have turned back at that point. In fact, we talked about it, but never seriously—I don't think. We clung with hope to the belief that God had led us to Kansas City for a reason, and we chose to trust Him to reveal it in His time. It wasn't easy, but we hung on.

As time went by, we began to see that God really did have a plan for our future. First He began to speak to each of us, through co-workers, mentors, and professors, about ministry to the military. Eventually we compared notes on the ideas God was planting in our heads and recognized Mike's call to Army Chaplaincy—a mission field in its own right. Shortly after that, God opened the door for me to become editorial assistant and then editor for some of our denomination's Sunday school curriculum. That's where my writing career began.

Looking back I realize that neither of these ministry opportunities would have been available to us in San Diego. From that location, we didn't even know they existed. But God had called us into the ministry, and He knew where He wanted us to start. God had a plan, and He faithfully worked it out.

Father, I love it when Your plans are revealed. I may not recognize them until I'm looking back at the work You've done, but help me to trust You just the same. Amen.

Discouraged Again

"May our Lord Jesus Christ himself and God our Father, who loved us and by his grace gave us eternal encouragement and good hope, encourage your hearts and strengthen you in every good deed and word." –2 Thessalonians 2:16-17

It happened again. I got lost. Then I drove around in circles until tears came to my eyes. By the time I found familiar territory and a road leading to my new home, I'd vowed to either move back to the old one or never leave the inside of the new one again. Of course, once I actually *arrived* at my new home, I realized that neither option was truly a possibility. I started the afternoon being discouraged that I'd become discouraged again.

Eventually, however, I admitted that I needed to spend some time talking to God about the hurts of my morning. I curled up on the couch with my favorite cozy blanket and told God all about my day. I confessed my frustration and discouragement. Then I asked Him to help me hang onto a more positive outlook next time—knowing that there *would* be a next time, unless I held myself to the rash promise to never leave the house again.

God showed me during that time of prayer that sometimes I'm just too hard on myself. I expect myself to be more than human and to respond to every crisis with a perfect attitude. But God is still at work, and I'm still a maturing child in His eyes. That means the next time I feel discouraged, instead of becoming even more discouraged because of my discouragement, I should turn to God first for comfort, for hope, for strength, and for that promised eternal encouragement. Eternal encouragement: it never runs out! God will offer it as often as I need it; He understands.

Thanks for strengthening my Spirit, Lord. Let's try this again! Amen.

157

Worry Won't Fix It

"Can any one of you by worrying add a single hour to your life?"
–Matthew 6:27

We had been living in our new home for almost a year, but one of our children was still having trouble adapting to his new environment. Friends hadn't come as easily as he had anticipated. The new school was more challenging. The teacher seemed unsympathetic. Our son came home with a new frustration every day.

At first I prayed for him, while doing what I could to help. Gradually, however, I became discouraged, too. My prayers changed to worries and desperate pleas for action on my child's behalf. Soon I was greeting this child at the door, not with a smile, but in anxious anticipation of the day's sad report.

One night, as I lay in bed pondering the especially troubling news of that day, God reminded me that worry shows a lack of trust. As I recognized this, He showed me how my worries could actually be adding to my child's burden instead of easing it. He also showed what worry was doing to me, sapping my strength as I poured more and more energy into it each day. "You don't have to worry," God seemed to whisper that night. "*I* will help your child through this difficult time." In those quiet moments of the night, I turned my son back over to Jesus and gratefully felt my heart fill with peace.

The next day, I happened to be driving past the school when I saw my son with a group of boys. They were talking and laughing, excited about something apparently good. "Thank You, Lord," I prayed, "for reassurance to go with Your peace."

When things seem dark, Father, remind me to leave my burdens with You. Worry can't change anything, but You can! Amen.

A Prayer for You

"I pray that out of his glorious riches he may strengthen you with power through his Spirit in your inner being." –Ephesians 3:16

Unbelievable! Twice in one day! I actually got lost twice in one day! Construction roadblocks sent me off into Never Land—the land from where I always think I'll never find my way home. I did find home, though. Both times! But I came home feeling shaky, vulnerable, tense, and afraid.

That's when I found this comforting verse. It seems Paul prayed for His spiritual children. Though the letter was addressed to the Ephesians, I believe the prayer continues for you and for me. Paul prayed that God would dig into his glorious storehouse of riches to give us everything we need to continue on confidently in this uncertain life. (Am I elaborating too much? I don't think so.) He prayed that God would strengthen us from the inside out through his Spirit, the One Jesus called, "the Comforter." With all of that, we no longer have any reason to feel shaky, vulnerable, tense, or afraid.

So as I write this, I'm thinking of you. And while I'm thinking of you, I'll take a moment to pray: May God do the same for you—and more—as He's done for me today.

Father, please send Your Spirit to comfort, encourage, and strengthen us all as we face the daily struggles of an ever-changing life. Thank You for generously providing all we need and so much more. Amen.

Pass It On

"Praise be to the God and Father of our Lord Jesus Christ, the Father of compassion and the God of all comfort, who comforts us in all our troubles, so that we can comfort those in any trouble with the comfort we ourselves receive from God." –2 Corinthians 1:3-4

Driving in Europe is intimidating—even in those countries where people drive on the right side of the road. There are many strange road signs, markings, and rules of the road. Learning who has the right of way in any given situation is the biggest challenge of all.

As a result, one of our first challenges upon moving to the Netherlands was to pass a notoriously difficult written driving test. Several people told us the same thing, "Don't feel bad if you don't pass the first time. Lots of people fail." Then they'd add, "Of course, *I* didn't." Passing became a matter of pride as well as a challenge.

I was terrified, but managed to pass in spite of my nerves. People said I was ready for the road; I didn't agree. It was another week before I worked up the courage to drive. I was sure that accidents, tickets, and eternal loss of direction waited around every curve of the winding roads. They didn't. (Well, loss of direction did. But it wasn't eternal.) Once I got behind the wheel, I learned it wasn't so bad. Now I have trouble remembering why I was so afraid.

A few months later, I ran into a friend from New York whose husband had just been stationed in Germany. She was facing the same driving test and was equally terrified. "I'll never be able to drive in this country, Janet!" she moaned.

Thanks to my experience, I was able to take her by the shoulders, look into her eyes, and say, "Yes. You will. You're going to be just fine. You can do this." Then we prayed for each other, and we still do.

God of all comfort, thank You for helping me through challenging situations. When I meet friends facing similar trials, show me how to pass along the comfort I've received from You, so we both can benefit. Without You we're lost, but with You and each other, we're strong. Amen.

Finding the Path

"You make known to me the path of life; you will fill me with joy in your presence, with eternal pleasures at your right hand."
—Psalm 16:11

As I've already mentioned, travel in the Netherlands was confusing at first. No grid. No North, South, East, or West signs. Frequent detours. Twisty roads. Often I'd head out in one direction convinced I was driving *away* from my destination, only to find myself just where I wanted to be. To this day, I'm convinced Maastricht is both to the West and to the North of where we lived because I could get there going either direction on the freeway. What a mystery!

Once I understood the road sign system, however, travel became much easier. It didn't matter if I was traveling North, South, East, or West. I just had to find a blue sign with the name of the city I hoped to reach and go in the direction it told me to. I'd stay on the road the sign put me on *no matter which way it twisted or turned* until I saw a sign telling me to go another way. If I kept following the little blue city signs, I'd always get where I wanted to go.

God reveals His path for our lives in much the same way. He doesn't hand us a road map at birth telling us how to get from point A to point B. We can't look ahead and chart our own course. Instead, we must follow the signs, one at a time, turning only when the signs say turn. If we stray off the path, God will point out new signs leading to the original destination from our new location. The key is to watch for the signs, following with trust and joy.

Father, the signs don't always seem to be right. But You know the terrain much better than I. I'll trust Your way. Amen.

162

Chapter 9
Discovering Community

Sowing Righteousness

"Sow righteousness for yourselves, reap the fruit of unfailing love, and break up your unplowed ground; for it is time to seek the Lord, until he comes and showers righteousness on you."
–Hosea 10:12

Let's use our imaginations for a moment today. Begin by picturing a young farmer back in the days of the pioneers. He's just purchased his first plot of land—several promising acres. He stands at the edge of the space he plans to turn into his first fruitful field of crops, puts one hand on his hip, and shades his eyes with the other. Looking out over the land, he pictures his dream come true—tall and healthy corn, wheat, or hay, ready for the harvest.

Yet he knows his dream won't come true until he gets to work. He clears the field of rocks that may get in his way and damage his equipment. He breaks the ground, making long furrows that stretch from one end of the designated area to the other. Then he sows the seed and begins to care for it daily, trusting God for the harvest of his dreams. Farming is a risky business, so he knows things may or may not go as he plans, but he also knows that God is in control. That's good enough for him. He's willing to do his part.

Now imagine that your new community is your field. Like the farmer, you have dreams, and you hope they will come true. But they won't come true until you get to work.

First, clear the land of your fears, prejudices, and pre-conceived expectations. These can get in your way and damage your ability to do God's will. Next, break up the ground: learn your way around, meet people, get involved where God directs. Now you are ready to sow seeds of righteousness. Smile. Treat people kindly. Show God's love wherever you go. In His time, God will shower the same back on you, and you'll find you live in a fruitful land.

Father, show me where to sow those seeds. I'm preparing a harvest for You! *Amen.*

Always Home

"I rejoiced with those who said to me, 'Let us go to the house of the Lord.'" –Psalm 122:1

Just before our family moved from Maine to New York, we contacted the pastor of our denomination's church in what would be our new town. On the day we moved in, he showed up on our doorstep to introduce himself and ask if we needed any help. We did! We were trying to unload the moving truck ourselves, but the piano and sofa bed were not cooperating with the narrow porch steps. Within a few hours, our new friend had rounded up several more new friends, who not only helped us with the big stuff, but also stayed to unpack the whole truck.

A few days later, the "storm of the century" hit our new town, knocking out all electricity for miles around. Our home was without power for eight days in the middle of winter. Knowing we hadn't had time to shop, several people from the church came to check on us. Their gifts of candles, groceries, firewood and batteries helped us through that challenging time.

The following Sunday was a day of rejoicing and celebration among the members of that church. People shared testimony after testimony of how God had provided for them, so they could provide for each other through the storm. Our family was new to the area, but one place already felt like home.

Father, thank You for Your church. Wherever I go, lead me to Your people. As I find my place among them, show me how to love them as they've loved me. Amen.

Finding the Familiar

"Be strong and courageous. Do not be afraid or terrified because of them, for the Lord your God goes with you; he will never leave you nor forsake you." –Deuteronomy 31:6

Finding one's place in a new neighborhood can be a frightening task. At first, the people of the community are "them," and "they" are scary. God assures us that He won't leave us to face "them" alone, however. He commands us to not be afraid or terrified. He'll go with us. He'll hold our hands, but we must obey and choose to be strong.

Where should we start, though? For me, one of the least intimidating ways to move from an "us/them" mentality to "us/us" is to find my favorite familiar places in "their" community and make them mine, too. For example, almost all communities have libraries—and I *love* libraries. Walking into a new library and getting my own library card associates me with "them" and helps me feel like I belong. The "walking in" part is challenging, but God goes with me, and we almost always come out triumphantly. (Once, I went in so quickly that I didn't have proof of my new address yet. I had to make a second trip to get that all-important card. I didn't give up, though. Neither should you.)

Other ideas include learning your way around the local mall, finding your very own hairdresser, and eating at a local franchise of a favorite restaurant. What are your favorite things to do that can be done in any community? Make a list, then take that first bold step. With God by your side, you'll learn that "they" are a lot like you. Soon you'll begin to belong.

Father, help me to stop seeing "them" as "them." I want us to be "us." Lead me to familiar places in this strange space, and give me the courage to walk in and conquer. Amen.

Books in Progress

"Don't grumble against one another, brothers and sisters, or you will be judged. The Judge is standing at the door!" –James 5:9

It can be hard not to grumble when someone you meet behaves differently than you expect, perhaps in a way you don't approve of. This is especially challenging if you've moved into a community where the entire culture behaves much differently than what you've defined as the norm. Yet God commands us not to grumble. This means don't complain about others aloud to your family or close friends. Harder still, it means don't even grumble to yourself. "The Judge is standing at the door!"—and He can read your mind.

So what can we do when we're tempted to grumble? Try thinking of the people you meet as books in progress. God has set many stories in motion. He's given each one a will of its own, so that each one is trying to write itself. Those of us who are Christians have realized we need God's authorship. We've given control of the story back to Him—or at least we're making every effort to leave that control in His hands day by day. The more we practice and obey, the easier and more automatic this becomes. Others are still trying to write their stories themselves. They've yet to discover or confess their absolute need for God.

Just as we'd never judge the quality of a book before it was completed, we don't have the right to judge the quality of a person either. In light of this fresh understanding, we patiently lift those around us in prayer and wait for God's work to be done. Who knows? He may even let us contribute to the storyline of another person's life. That's hard to do well if we're grumbling.

Master Storyteller, I'm excited to see how great Your storylines will be. Help me wait with patience and expectation, not frustration or dislike. Amen.

Seizing Opportunity

**"Therefore, as we have opportunity, let us do good to all people,
especially to those who belong to the family of believers."
–Galatians 6:10**

One summer, our chapel was making last minute preparations for the annual Vacation Bible School program when a new family arrived in town. Hearing that the VBS staff was extremely short-handed, to the point that there was talk of canceling the program altogether, this family (a father, mother, and two teenagers) joined right in to fill four crucial staff spots. They were living in a hotel and hadn't even begun to search for a home for themselves, yet they graciously put their plans on hold to help the family of believers as they could.

While it's true that we should usually settle in and seek God's will before making long-term commitments within our new communities, this doesn't mean that we can't eagerly jump in to help with smaller projects as opportunities arise. Vacation Bible School only lasts a week, and some roles require no preparation at all. Has the nursery worker called in sick for the day? Sitting with babies is a needed ministry, as well as an opportunity to pray for the little ones in your care. Perhaps people are signing up to take meals to the sick or to shut-ins. Even if your cooking equipment isn't unpacked quite yet, you can grab a bucket of chicken with a few fixin's and go on an adventure to make a new friend. Opportunities are all around. Ask God to show you where you can help.

Lord, people react with surprise and joy when a newcomer starts right in doing good. This makes the effort more fun. Show me where I can help today. Let me seize that opportunity and make the most of it for You. Amen.

The Commissary

"Therefore I tell you, do not worry about your life, what you will eat or drink; or about your body, what you will wear. Is not life more important than food, and the body more important than clothes?" –Matthew 6:25

When our family lived in the Netherlands, a friend of mine shared a sweet lesson in contentment. When she first moved to the Netherlands, she was disappointed in the small commissary (a military grocery store) on the small American post. She didn't know how she'd ever find what she needed for her family in that place. She soon learned, though, that the commissary provided more than enough. In fact, the manager even took special requests, attempting to help Americans feel more at home.

Knowing that, and discovering all the native specialties available at Dutch markets, our families actually had the best of both worlds. God provided through both the commissary and the market, and He provided abundantly. There was no need for worry. We had access to more than enough.

How spoiled we were, though! Worrying about whether or not we'd have access to American favorites like turkey or corn on the cob. God has promised to provide what we need, and what we need most is life—eternal life!—not food or clothes. Again, God has provided abundantly. Thanks to Jesus, those who believe are not only saved, but also adopted as His children. Our lives are in God's hands.

Gracious Heavenly Father, thank You for showing me what I should be most thankful for. There's no need to worry when You're in control. Thank You so much! Amen.

A Table of Experience

"You prepare a table before me in the presence of my enemies."
–Psalm 23:5

My husband loves to sample exotic dishes in off-the-beaten-path restaurants. He has no qualms about walking into an unfamiliar place and ordering something unusual off the menu. I prefer the same tried and true item from the same tried and true restaurant *every* time. Forget exploring! Take me to McDonald's and get me a Big Mac.

Thankfully, Mike insists on a compromise here. Once in a while, we go to the same old favorite place where I can relax and enjoy the same comfortable meal yet again, while Mike scans the menu for something he's never tried before. Other times, we go somewhere *semi-exotic* (I have my limits) where Mike can eat mushrooms the size of hamburgers with goat cheese on the side, while I scrutinize the menu for something not-too-risky. As a result, I now sometimes long for curry sauce-covered chicken and rice. I know that peanut sauce isn't much different than peanut butter—and it doesn't taste so good on sautéed vegetables and beef. Dutch meatballs in mystery gravy and cranberry sauce are fairly tasty. Focaccia (an Italian bread) is edible in a pinch.

While it's true that not all new dishes have appealed to me, I've appreciated trying them after all. My life has been enhanced by a touch of variety. Just the same, my life has been enriched by the experiences God has dished out through each move. Though I've often asked if He'd mind if I just stay in the same old place and do the same old thing, God knows I need more than that. In each new home, He gently teaches and treats. Sometimes I feel I'm in the presence of mine enemies when, in reality, I'm only among strangers who are about to become friends. God knows that sharing the banquet will bond us in His ever-wondrous way. He knows what's best for me. I'm glad He puts it on my plate.

Father, You've prepared an enticing meal. I'm ready to eat. Amen.

Rescued and Enabled

"The oath he swore to our father Abraham: to rescue us from the hand of our enemies, and to enable us to serve him without fear in holiness and righteousness before him all our days." –Luke 1:73-75

Claiming God's promise to Abraham allows us to move into new communities with confidence. Step one is asking God to rescue us from our enemies. These aren't human enemies like the ones the Israelites faced. Our enemies may include fear, discontentment, homesickness, disillusionment, frustration, and perhaps even anger. Depending on your unique situation, you may be able to think of others. Our enemies are the attitudes and emotions that fester within, effectively keeping us from settling into our new homes peacefully. Ask God to help you identify them, so you'll know what He's rescuing you from.

That leads me to step two. We don't just ask God to chase our enemies away; we ask Him to replace them with something positive. For example, once God rescues us from fear, He makes room for confidence—which enables us to serve Him "in holiness and righteousness before him all our days." Likewise, removing homesickness makes room for a fresh appreciation of all that surrounds us now. Removing frustration makes room for patience, and so on. God's removing the bad makes room for His gift of the enabling good. Once that's in place, we can serve our Savior in a perfect, pure, and right way.

Father, please identify and remove the enemy within—anything that keeps me from serving You as I long to do. Make me able to do Your will in this new place. Thank You, Lord! Amen.

Aliens

"Consequently, you are no longer foreigners and strangers, but fellow citizens with God's people and also members of God's household."–Ephesians 2:19

One of the first things we had to do once we arrived in the Netherlands was register as aliens. We laughed all the way to the police station and all the way home. We were legal aliens—officially so. We even had little pink cards to carry in our wallets reminding us that this was so.

While we lived there, however, we encountered other reminders of our alien status *daily*. The announcer on the radio spoke in Dutch. Signs were written in something that looked like gibberish to me. The rules of the road were unfamiliar and sometimes confusing. People dressed and ate differently, and the list went on. No matter how welcome I felt in that strange land, my surroundings wouldn't let me forget I was an alien.

Whenever I experience this feeling that I don't quite belong, it is comforting to know that I'm a card-carrying citizen of God's kingdom. He's preparing a place for me that includes a home and heavenly clothes. And while I wait, He's teaching me the language of perfect love.

When I feel like a stranger, I focus on my king. Among God's people, I always belong.

Thank You, Lord, for citizenship in Your growing kingdom here and that perfect Country above. Amen.

Let the Oxen Eat!

"Do not muzzle an ox while it is treading out the grain."
–Deuteronomy 25:4

This verse tickles my funny bone. I accidentally memorized it the first time I read it, not because I was immediately struck by its wealth of spiritual value, but simply because it made me laugh. It seems absurd that God had Moses put such a trivial rule right in the middle of a list of regulations for getting along with other people! But there it is—must be important somehow.

Picture the scene, the oxen are hooked up to the treadmill, walking around in circles. Their heads are down in despair as they trudge along because they are surrounded by food they can't eat. Muzzles have been placed over their ever-watering mouths. Don't you feel sorry for the poor, hard-working, uncompensated beasts?

Now picture yourself in their place. Doesn't life sometimes seem like such a treadmill? You settle in, learn your way around, make friends, pack, say good-bye, drive off, and start all over again—and again and again. What drudgery! How pointless!

But it isn't pointless. If God cares enough about a couple of oxen to tell their owners to let them eat while they work, you can be sure that He's going to let you enjoy life on the treadmill, too. There's no muzzle on your mouth to keep you from enjoying all God has to offer in each place. Make friends, see sights, create memories, and thank God for it all. Don't let yourself get so caught up in the task that you miss out on all the fun. Lift your head and look around. Life on the treadmill with God can be great!

Father, what treats have you hidden in the business of this day? I'm looking around. Thank You, Lord!

Blessed Wherever

"You will be blessed in the city and blessed in the country."
–Deuteronomy 28:3

"I'll never get used to this city," said my new friend, Laurette.

"What city?" I asked. We laughed. Laurette came from a small, rural town with maybe one stoplight. I come from a rolling suburb in California where it's difficult to know where one city ends and another begins. From my perspective, our corner of Kansas City was a small, rural town. Laurette felt she'd moved to downtown Manhattan. Yet both of us found our new home to feel a bit foreign.

As the Israelites prepared to move into Canaan, God told them that if they obeyed Him, He'd bless them. (See Deut. 28:1-14.) If they disobeyed, a harsh curse would be the consequence. (See verses 15-68.) The lesson for us is that God expects His people to obey.

As we begin to explore our new surroundings, whether city, country, suburb, metropolis, or hermit's cave, our goal should always be the same, to love, obey, and glorify our God. He's the same wherever we are. His expectations stay the same, too, clearly spelled out in His Word. Discover them to obey them. Seek God with all your heart and you'll be blessed—wherever.

Father, the blessings of peace, contentment, hope, and joy are precious to me wherever I go. My obedience seems a small price for all that comes with knowing You. I gladly seek Your will. Amen.

Check the Source

"Don't be deceived, my dear brothers and sisters." –James 1:16

I just deleted twenty people from my family tree. They were people I'd come to know and love, but they had to go. With a click of the mouse and a few keystrokes, not only were they gone, but replaced with fresh faces (in my imagination). Now they're new people I'll look forward to getting to know. They have a place in my history, after all.

No. I am not disowning my relatives. I learned I'd been deceived. While examining one branch of the family tree, I discovered a mistake. My source said that Margaret's parents were William and Elizabeth. Other sources said her parents were James and Frances. I checked my source; it wasn't very strong. I checked their sources: undeniable! Goodbye William, Elizabeth, and your ancestors. Hello James and Frances. Welcome to my tree! I'm sure Margaret is thankful I fixed *that* mistake.

Just as a genealogist has to be careful not to accept everything she hears or reads as the truth, Christians must do the same. As you join a new community, you are bound to hear new ideas: through the local media, through new friends, perhaps even through your church. Examine these carefully. Ask God to reveal His Truth, and seek it through His Word. Once someone leads you down the wrong path, correcting your course isn't as simple as clicking a mouse. Don't be deceived. Go to the Source.

Father, when I encounter contradictions, help me to find resolutions through You. Only Your Truth is absolute. Don't let me become confused. Amen.

Ambassadors

"We are therefore Christ's ambassadors, as though God were making his appeal through us." –2 Corinthians 5:20

By definition, an ambassador is someone who travels to a foreign country as a representative of his own country's interests. A good ambassador meets with foreign leaders face to face in order to get to know them, to experience their culture, to understand them, and to befriend them, that when negotiations are necessary, two countries can come to the table with some positive history on the books and common ground under their feet. For this reason, an ambassador who never left his country of birth would fail at this crucial point in time.

In a sense, Christ was God's ambassador to humankind. He left His kingdom to experience ours; and He experienced it fully from babyhood to His death. In doing so, He made it possible for us to join His kingdom. After rising from death, He commissioned His followers to spread the Word. Then He returned to Heaven, leaving us as His representatives here on Earth. We *are* His ambassadors to the unsaved of this world.

Granted, He calls some of His ambassadors to minister to those who physically live nearby, yet spiritually live outside the kingdom. Yes, we're talking about two different realms. Yet as we moving ambassadors face relocation, it's exciting to think of each as a Divine appointment. As I experience each new community, I get to know new people and allow them to know me. Somewhere in this process, if I'm faithful to God, they'll get to know Him, too—at least they'll see Him living in me. They'll know whose kingdom I belong to, that when we come to the table, they'll be ready to hear Christ's appeal. Moving's a great privilege from that point of view.

Lord of All, prepare the hearts of new neighbors I'll meet. Make me ready to represent You. Amen.

God's Expansion Plan

"Whoever serves me must follow me; and where I am, my servant also will be. My Father will honor the one who serves me."
–John 12:26

While stationed in Korea, a friend became involved in an excellent youth ministry mentoring program. He and his wife both learned how the program worked, became leaders in it, and led many youth into a deeper walk with Christ.

Shortly after his transfer to the Netherlands, our friend began talking with leaders of this ministry still in Korea about starting a new branch of the program in Europe. The leaders enthusiastically vowed their support. In fact, once our friend arranged the details through our military chapel and set a launch date, several leaders *and* teens from the Korean branch traveled to the Netherlands at their own expense to help. Several months later, teens mentored in that initial meeting worked with our friend to hold another meeting to reach a new group. My teenage son was among those eager young servants.

God is in Korea. God is in the Netherlands. Using the military as a vehicle, He moved our friend from one to the other to expand His work among national and military youth living on opposite sides of the world. Our friend served and followed, and God has honored him with success.

Father, You are so wise to use the circumstances of Your obedient servants' lives to expand Your kingdom as You will. Use me, too! Amen.

Chicken Talk

**"Rejoice always; pray continually, give thanks in all circumstances;
for this is God's will for you in Christ Jesus."**
–1 Thessalonians 5:16-18

Culture shock is a reality that we movers have to face whether we move across town, across the country, or around the world. While adjusting to a new community, it's tempting to play the compare and contrast game. "My old church did that this way, and it was so much more effective." "My old grocery store had lower prices and more to choose from." "The ladies in the PTA back home were friendlier." No matter how you felt about your old home, there will be times when the grass seemed to be greener there.

Opening my first carton of eggs in a Dutch market was such an experience for me. Instead of finding pretty white eggs, polished to perfection and stamped with the USDA seal of approval, I found eggs covered with feathers and "stuff."

My husband laughed at me. "You didn't think eggs come out of chickens clean, did you?" I'm a city girl, I did, and that's how I wanted to find my eggs at the store.

But God doesn't want us to compare and contrast. He wants us to be joyful in our present circumstance. If we pray continually, He'll fill our heart with *His* joy. We may have to make a few adjustments along the way, like learning to wash our own eggs, but there will always be something to be thankful for. I recommend Dutch chocolates, cheeses, and breads!

Lord, I'm adjusting to this new place. Help me to ignore its frustrations while joyfully discovering its treasures. Thank you for this new circumstance of my life. Amen.

Meeting Together

"And let us not neglect our meeting together, as some people do, but encourage one another." –Hebrews 10:25, NLT

When Mike and I moved to Kansas City, we both were faced with finding a new church home for the first time. Our parents made the decision for us when we were children. In college, we attended with friends. In Kansas City, however, we had to summon up our courage and walk in as strangers. This was frightening for me.

The first church we attended was very small. We had a new baby and were concerned about nursery care—our new-parent standards were pretty high. The church people were welcoming and friendly, but seemed so eager to add a young family to their membership that I think they scared us off.

The second church was a little bit bigger and a little bit colder. We felt intimidated somehow. Nursery care was still a concern. We decided to try one more church.

This third was so huge that it had five nurseries! Yet the workers still managed to switch our child's bottle with another's. We felt somewhat lost among all the people until we found a friendly couple. They introduced us to others. After talking the matter over, we decided we were tired of looking for the perfect church. We stayed right where we were.

Over our time in Kansas City, though, I made friends with several people from the first two churches. I know now that we would have been just as happy at either place. Perhaps God led us to the third church, or perhaps that's just where we happened to end our search. What mattered was that we'd overcome fear and found a church home.

We worshipped with others, grew in our Christian walk, and helped as we could. We didn't use moving as an excuse to give up.

Father, please lead me to the church where You want me to grow and serve. Give me courage to start visiting right away. Amen.

Foreign Songs

"How can we sing the songs of the Lord while in a foreign land?"
–Psalm 137:4

Shortly before our first Christmas in the Netherlands, I attended a ladies' retreat in Willingen, Germany. We spent most of our time attending workshops and worship services within the confines of the resort and, so, were not exposed to the German culture much. We were Americans among Americans for the greater part of the week.

On the last day, however, a sweet, German woman took us on a walking tour of her village. She told us a little about its history and how it came to be the resort town it is today. Our last stop on the tour was a small, but modern, church. Walking in, I didn't see much difference between this church and the American ones I've known, which is unusual in Europe—a continent full of both grand cathedrals and modest brick buildings that outdate the USA.

Our tour group took seats near the front, and I began to look around. Written decoratively on the walls were several Scripture verses. Remembering what I could from high school and college, I translated enough to recognize the familiar and beloved words of the Lord's Prayer. Our tour guide asked us to name a few favorite hymns and choruses. Then she led us to their German words in the hymnals. Our pronunciation wasn't perfect, but we were able to sing "He's Got the Whole World in His Hands" and "Silent Night" in a *foreign* tongue that day. How did we do this? We opened our mouths to worship our God, just like we do when we're home.

Father, thank You that people all over the world can worship You, our one, true God, regardless of language or place. It's a privilege to share the song. Amen.

Just Passing Through

***"But you will receive power when the Holy Spirit comes on you; and you will be my witnesses in Jerusalem, and in all Judea and Samaria, and to the ends of the earth."* –Acts 1:8**

Jesus didn't say that it would be nice *if* we'd be His witnesses. He said that the Holy Spirit *will* come on us, and that we *will* be His witnesses . . . "to the ends of the earth." This is something that *will* happen, period, no discussion. I think, no, I'm certain, Christ expects us to cooperate. We movers have that "to the ends of the earth" part down. Now we just have to learn how to rely on the Holy Spirit's power to make us into Christ's witnesses.

William Penn once said, "I expect to pass through this world but once. Any good I can do, or any kindness that I can show, let me do now, for I shall not pass this way again." What a beautiful mission statement for life! If we edit it just a tad for movers, it becomes a very useful key to this witnessing thing as well. "I expect to pass through this [community] but once . . ." In other words, knowing that I'll only live in this God-chosen place for a short time, I must rely on His Spirit to show me what good I can do, what kindness I can show. If I obey the Spirit, my life will naturally become a witness to the people impacted by my actions. As we get to know each other, God's Spirit may even give me that privileged opportunity to lead some of those people to Christ. It all begins with goodness, kindness, and obedience to God.

Lord, as You send me to the ends of the earth, let my actions reveal an image of You. I'm eager to be Your witness. Amen.

People Are People Wherever You Go

"There is neither Jew nor Gentile, neither slave nor free, nor is their male and female, for you are all one in Christ Jesus."
–Galatians 3:28

As a minister's wife, I've lived in eight states and the Netherlands, but I still think of myself as a Californian—proudly, in fact. Wherever I go, however, I hear all kinds of interesting comments about stereotypical Californians. Some people just love to tell displaced Californians what's wrong with the state they are from, yet these seem not to notice that I don't fit the mold. (I guess they figure since I don't live there anymore, I've recovered.) But my friends and family still living in California don't fit the mold either. Believe it or not, a lot of devoted Christians live in that state—and they don't do drugs or carry guns in their cars to shoot each other with on the freeway. Some even vote for Republicans!

Living in other states, however, I've discovered some misconceptions of my own. Not all Mainers like lobster and Upstate New Yorkers tend to be different from the stereotypical city folk—who may not all be stereotypical. I've even met a few Texans who don't feel obligated to display their state star. When I left the country, I learned that Germans don't wear Lederhosen very often and most Dutch people have given up the wooden shoes.

The point is: people are people. Most are happy to return a simple smile. Most are eager to make friends. Most just want to be accepted and loved and known for whom they are—not what they look like or where they happen to live. God made each individual from a unique mold, and He loves each one. Further, He's bonded all Christians together as brothers and sisters in Christ. We're a unified family; we're meant to get along.

Father, as I move from location to location, help me to approach each individual with an open mind and an eager heart to get to know the person inside. Thank You! Amen.

The Key to Being Content

"For I have learned to be content whatever the circumstances."
–Philippians 4:11

I think the most likely cause of stress for me during the holidays is learning to let go of or be flexible with traditions. As we move from place to place, ministry situation to ministry situation, sometimes traditions conflict with cultural situations or ministry expectations. As a result, I've had to learn to adjust or be sad. I've come to see that being sad is, sometimes, a silly thing to do.

Here's an example: for the first few years of my marriage, I insisted on making peas every Thanksgiving.

"Honey, we don't like peas," Mike would say. "Why do you make them?"

My answer was that Thanksgiving wasn't Thanksgiving without peas. My grandmother had made them every year. After a few successive years of throwing away almost full dishes of the roly poly vegetable, though, I finally tried Thanksgiving dinner without the peas. We did not miss them. In fact, we were thankful to see them go.

Similarly, my family of origin always watched football on New Year's Day, yet neither my husband nor I watch football. (It's only fun if my dad is there.) When we left California and celebrated our first New Year's away from home, I felt like something was missing. We didn't want to watch football, though, so we've invented our own family traditions for that day.

The adaptation process really got complicated when my husband and I joined the military community and found ourselves in a whole new world of traditions for holidays: attending chapel services at the time we would traditionally eat dinner or open gifts, eating in the dining facility on a holiday, and contributing to the occasional potluck meal to celebrate as a community. All of these are good—and even enjoyable. But they weren't our traditions, so accepting the change was a challenge. Because holidays are celebrated differently in every location, I've learned flexibility is the key. The military is our place of ministry; I'm happier serving God than clinging to traditions that don't need to be.

Paul is my example in this. Near the end of his letter to the Philippians, he thanks those dear people for their concern about his troubles and assures them that he has learned to be content in whatever circumstances God puts him in. From prison to palaces, Paul has known it all. He takes life as it comes, praising God in very situation. I want to learn to do this, too.

So, to avoid stress through the holidays, we learn what events to prepare for, plan our traditions around them, let go of the non-essentials, and enjoy celebrating with whoever is around. Most important, we worship God, offering Him thanks and spending time in reflection, wonder and awe. Remembering Him wherever we are is the key to being content.

Thank You, Father, for the blessing of family and friends. As we gather together wherever we are, may we find contentment in You. Amen.

God's Unchanging Law

"Your decrees are the theme of my song wherever I lodge."
–Psalm 119:54

Every time we move to a new city, we have to take the time to learn its laws. Are U-turns legal? Up to what age and weight do children have to ride in car seats? If we homeschool our kids, what does the state require from us? Can I turn right on a red light? What do I have to recycle and what can I throw away? The list goes on and on. Finding the answers takes time. Neglecting to do so can result in a costly fine.

Thankfully, God's law never changes. Micah summed it up in a few short lines: "He has showed you, O man, what is good. And what does the Lord require of you? To act justly and to love mercy and to walk humbly with your God" (6:8). Jesus condensed it further: "'Love the Lord your God with all your heart and with all your soul and with all your mind.' This is the first and greatest commandment. And the second is like it: 'Love your neighbor as yourself'" (Matthew 22:37-38).

So simple! Love God. Love your neighbor—wherever you go.

Lord, Make Your love the theme of my song wherever I lodge. Amen.

Chapter 10
Reaching Out to Neighbors

Volunteering

"Then I heard the voice of the Lord saying, 'Whom shall I send? And who will go for us?' And I said, 'Here am I. Send me!'"
–Isaiah 6:8

My husband and I used to watch a television program called *Quantum Leap*. In this program, the star of the show, a lonely scientist whose experiment had gone dreadfully wrong, found himself leaping through time into the lives of different people. In order to leap to the next life, he had to fix something that the person had done wrong—he had to restore time and make life better. This scientist didn't go enthusiastically, though. With each leap, he hoped his next would take him home. In the final episode, however, he realized that leaping through time, fixing lives along the way, was his great contribution to humanity. He decided to continue.

When we move, we have a similar choice. We can reluctantly let others drag us from place to place and resolutely do what needs to be done. Or we can enthusiastically embark on a new adventure, asking God to show us ways to build His kingdom along the way. Maybe there is a task that needs to be completed and your unique combination of talents is just right for the job. Or maybe you are uniquely able to minister to someone with a specific need because of experiences you've had in other places. Maybe your next-door neighbor needs to hear the gospel from a fresh perspective—yours!

When God was looking for someone to send to His people, Isaiah volunteered. In fact, if you look at the end of the sentence showing his response, you'll see an exclamation point. Isaiah earnestly wanted to do something for God. We can serve God, too!

I'm sorry that I'm not always excited about moving, Lord. Please help me to see unique opportunities in each place. Lead me to the people You'd have me serve for You. Here I am. Send me!

Pleasing the Neighbor

"Each of us should please our neighbors for their good, to build them up." –Romans 15:2

When we moved into our home in the Netherlands, the previous tenant told us that one of the neighbors had continually tried to talk him into giving up his gas-powered lawn mower. "You should use a push mower," he'd say. "Good exercise!" What he meant was, "Much quieter!" Dutch people value peace in their neighborhoods. I never once heard the sound of a lawn mower while we lived in that home.

Our yard was big, though, and Mike didn't look forward to mowing it the old-fashioned way. We'd left our electric mower in the States because we knew it would be tough to make it run on a European power supply, so Mike headed to the store to see what he could find. I was very surprised when he came back with a simple push-mower, borrowed from Army Community Services for three years. After considering the cost of an electric mower (considerably higher than expected) and the neighbor's request, Mike decided he could manage on human energy for a few years—with the help of a growing, teenage son. Our neighbor was pleased, it was for *all* our good, and our son got to be built up!

Thank You for our new neighbors, Lord. Show us how to live among them as a positive influence toward their ultimate good—a life being built up in You. Amen.

Holey Knees

"Who is wise and understanding among you? Let them show it by their good life, by deeds done in the humility that comes from wisdom." –James 3:13

The three boys living in my household were God's gift to me and my husband for a time. They were a privilege, a blessing, and a trust. They were also a wacky and wild adventure, something I would never trade. But my boys didn't always help me make the best, first impression in a strange, new place.

For example, when Justin was little, I dropped him off in the toddler nursery one Sunday. He looked adorable with his hair slicked back, suspenders and bow tie in place, shirt tucked in—a little gentleman. When I picked him up, however, the gentleman was gone. In his place was an imp with loose suspenders, an untucked shirt, and hair—well, let's not talk about his hair. Another parent looked from his still-pristine son to my ragamuffin and said, "You didn't bring him that way, did you?" I didn't answer—just took my boy and went home.

At a later time, I was sitting in our new dentist's office with my middle son, then ten. I happened to glance down at his knees and noticed with horror that they were missing! I tried, I really did. But Alex went through the knees of his jeans so fast I couldn't keep up. And he never bothered to tell me when they needed to be replaced because he preferred comfy, worn-in-worn-out jeans to new ones. If *I* failed to notice the holes, they grew. Thankfully, our dentist seemed to understand, and even appreciate, active little boys.

Needless to say, I didn't always have control over the impressions my children made, but I do have a measure of control over myself. As I move from place to place, I pray that people will see God's love shining through my life—and overlook any holey knees.

Father, today I ask for wisdom. Inspire my words and deeds. Let people see what You want them to—toward Your glory, Lord. Amen.

Timidity

"For God has not given us a spirit of fear and timidity, but of power, love, and self-discipline" –2 Timothy 1:7, NLT

I'll admit it. I'm timid by nature. Some call it shy. I prefer timid. Rabbits are considered timid, and people like rabbits. Whatever *you* choose to call it, I know it isn't something God planned for me. It's part of that fallen, sin-nature thing we all despise but can't defeat on our own. It's something I have to rely on God to help me conquer day by day.

Timidity is especially difficult in someone who moves often. Getting to know a new neighborhood and new neighbors takes courage. Driving around town in fear of getting lost takes courage. Walking up to a group of strangers in church or at a meeting to introduce oneself takes courage, too. Moving requires all of these actions; moving requires that one be brave.

That's why I like 2 Timothy 1:7. God did not give any of us a spirit of timidity. He gives us power, love, and self-discipline—everything we need to move successfully. Some versions of the Bible say "a sound mind" instead of "self-discipline." This is true as well. As I triumphantly drive from one location to another in my new town, I experience freedom and joy. Hiding in my house in fear would surely drive me insane.

Thank You, Lord, for the gifts my spirit needs to survive each move: power, love, self-discipline, and a sound mind. Help me always remember to exchange my timid spirit for the spirit You intended. Amen.

Operation Fragrance

"But thanks be to God, who always leads us as captives in Christ's triumphal procession and uses us to spread the aroma of the knowledge of him everywhere." –2 Corinthians 2:14

Trees and other plants rely on small animals to help them survive. Bees carry pollen from flower to flower in Spring. Squirrels take acorns and other nuts from place to place. Birds move the seeds from fruit trees to new locations where there may be more room for seedlings to grow. In turn, the animals get the food they need from the plants. God planned for the plants and animals to help each other in this way.

In a similar way, we carry the fragrance of the knowledge of God with us wherever we go. We plant seeds of God's love in others, helping His kingdom to thrive. As we go where God leads, He goes with us, filling us with His Spirit, His strength. This is God's plan for us. We are triumphant so long as we rely on Him.

Holy Spirit, fill my life with the fragrance of Your love that others may know You wherever I go. Amen.

Accept Like Christ

"Accept one another, then, just as Christ accepted you, in order to bring praise to God." –Romans 15:7

Christ accepts each of us just as we are. He sees all of our flaws, failures, quirks, and sins. He doesn't like these, but He loves *us*. And because He loves us, He accepts us when we humbly present our lives to Him and submit to His authority as God. From then on, He begins to remake us in His Image, gently bringing out the best and removing the worst. His goal is to make us into the people we would have been had sin not corrupted our lives. This brings praise to God, as our lives become a living testimony of His grace.

Romans 15:7 tells us we are to accept one another as Christ accepted us. When God brings people into our lives, we need to show Christ's love regardless of obvious flaws, failures, quirks, and sins. If Jesus loves them, so can we, relying on His help. By accepting and loving people, we point them to Jesus as the Holy Spirit begins to draw them to God. Then God can begin to work in their lives as He continues to work in ours. Accepting others, showing God's love to all, brings glory to His name.

There's an added benefit for you: As you accept others, others will accept you. You'll find your place in your new community as you let God love through you.

Jesus, some people are hard to accept, but sometimes I am, too. Help me to remember this, that I may graciously accept others as You've accepted me. Thank You, Lord of All. Amen.

Blech!

"Keep all my decrees and laws and follow them, so that the land
where I am bringing you to live may not vomit you out."
–Leviticus 20:22

As I write these words, I'm fighting some sort of stomach flu. I feel nauseated and weak. I'm chilled all over. The thought of food is repulsive. You know the feeling. You just want to crawl into bed, pull the covers up to your chin, and sleep until the queasiness goes away. I don't think it's a coincidence that I came across this verse today.

God's words to the Israelites are blunt: "Follow the rules or your new land will throw up to get rid of you" (Janet's translation). As we move into a new land, the last thing we want to do is offend the people we'll meet there. Leviticus 20:22 is the key to finding acceptance and making new friends: follow God by obeying His Word.

But the Bible is full of rules! Thankfully, Micah narrowed them down for us: "He has shown you, O mortal, what is good. And what does the Lord require of you? To act justly and to love mercy and to walk humbly with your God" (Micah 6:8). In other words, treat others fairly, be forgiving (rather than critical) when you see their faults, and enjoy fellowship with your God, recognizing that He is your Lord, the One who's in control. To sin against others is to offend—the land will reject you. To find fault or criticize is to affront—people will avoid you. To live without God's love is futile—you'll never feel you belong. To follow and obey God, however, is to find full acceptance in Him and among His people wherever you go.

Father, show me how to live so that I won't offend or hurt others. I'll walk with You and follow Your Word. Thank You for acceptance and love. Amen.

The Spirit's Fruit

"But the Holy Spirit produces this kind of fruit in our lives: love, joy, peace, patience, kindness, goodness, faithfulness, gentleness, and self-control. There is no law against these things!"
—Galatians 5:22-23, NLT

Before we are saved, the Holy Spirit's job is to draw us to Christ. Once we receive Christ as our Savior and Lord, the Spirit's work changes. He begins to make us more like Christ. We recognize the fruit of His work in our lives as we become more loving, joyful, at peace, patient, kind, good, faithful, gentle, and self-controlled. This fruit cannot grow in a life full of sin. Once we confess our sins and turn our lives over to God, the Spirit can replace the sin with "good fruit" against which "there is no law."

God's Spirit uses the circumstances of our lives to nurture His fruit—if we let Him. For example, moving gives me an opportunity to show God's love to a whole new community of people, which will cause God's love in my life to grow. This produces joy. As I choose to trust God with the events of each move, He'll give me peace through whatever situation arises. I don't think I need to explain how a move can produce patience, but pray for plenty of it before each move. Kindness, goodness, gentleness, and self-control grow as I relate to people with God's love. Lastly, moving requires faithfulness to God, to my spouse, and to people I leave behind if I want ties to remain strong across the miles.

With each of these, however, I can choose not to let God's Spirit work. This produces the opposite of the good fruit, though. If I refuse to greet people with God's love, I'll be lonely and, perhaps, bitter. If I worry and fret or lose my temper, these take the place of joy, peace, patience, and self-control. God's Spirit is always at work, but I have to relax and *let* Him work in order for effective change to take place in my life.

Father, thank You for Your Holy Spirit and the work He is doing in my life. Forgive me when I take control and act in counterproductive ways. I want to become more like Christ. Help me to relax and let Your Spirit do His job. Amen.

Loving Foreigners

"And you are to love those who are foreigners, for you yourselves were foreigners in Egypt." –Deuteronomy 10:19

Being part of a military community, I'm never the newcomer for long. Within weeks, there are several families newer to the area than mine. I must move quickly from being welcomed to welcoming others. I've learned the effort is worth my time.

There are at least three good reasons for reaching out to the "foreigner" in your community. The first, and most important, is to honor and obey God. Bringing glory to your Maker's name is priority one. Putting aside your own newcomer needs in order to show compassion and love to another is a great way to do this, not to mention an act commanded by God.

Reason number two is that the newcomer needs to see a friendly face. She needs a welcoming hug or handshake from someone in her new home. She needs to know she'll find friendship and acceptance in this new land. Because you are experiencing the same feelings and needs, you are the best to offer this to her. She may see you as a mentor because you've been in the area longer, but together you can discover and explore.

This leads to reason number three: in being a friend, you may make a new friend. As you honor God and love your new neighbor, the blessings will multiply in your life, too. This shouldn't be your primary motive, but it is a side benefit you can't ignore. God loves you. He wants you to find happiness in your new community. Reach out to your fellow foreigner, and be foreigners no more.

Father, as I recognize each newcomer, give me courage to reach out with genuine love and concern. Show me what to offer. Use my life to meet a need. Amen.

No Pride in Harmony

"Live in harmony with one another. Do not be proud, but be willing to associate with people of low position. Do not be conceited." –Romans 12:16

"But this is how we solved that problem in Kansas City," I explained. "It worked so well. Won't you just try the idea?" I was sitting in on a Vacation Bible School committee meeting at our new church in Maine. The committee wasn't interested in my suggestion. They had their own plan—and it worked! Surprise! Sometimes there are two ways to do something right.

When moving to a new place, it's impossible not to compare. If you want to make friends, however, you'll need to keep these comparisons to yourself. People who've lived in one community all their lives don't want to hear that you think people in another community have a better way of doing things. Your opinion will sound prideful—conceited. When comparing communities, remember that the fact that they arrange or handle things differently doesn't mean you have to decide one way is better than the other and push for immediate change. The two communities are just different. *You* must be open to change.

This doesn't mean you can never share a good idea from a past home. It just means that you should take a gentle and loving approach if you do.

First, be certain your audience is open to alternatives. If they've already determined how to proceed, this may not be the case. Yet if they are just beginning to plan, your thoughts may be welcome indeed. If so, present the idea as a possible solution to a recognized problem. Then leave it in the hands of those who will decide. If they choose to try the idea, help them, being careful not to gloat about how well you've seen the plan work before. If they choose to do something else, however, don't take their decision personally. They only want what they believe is best—just as you do. As Paul said, "Live in harmony with one another." Sometimes this means loving your new neighbors as they are.

Lord, help me to see my new community through Your eyes. Show me how to work with new friends and neighbors for the best of all. Amen.

Chapter 11
Making Friends

Seeking Kindred Spirits

*"So God created mankind in his own image, in the image of God
he created them; male and female he created them."*
–Genesis 1:27

Lucy Maud Montgomery's classic character, Anne Shirley, longed for a bosom friend—a kindred spirit who would share her interests and dreams, listen to her imaginative stories, and go along with her wild schemes. She found such a friend in Diana, her childhood playmate while she lived in her well-known House of Green Gables.

Like Anne, I long to find a kindred spirit in each new home. Other military wives I know feel the same way. In fact, at a recent get-to-know-you event, guests were asked to answer several questions about themselves including, "Who is your best friend?" One woman replied, "Which one shall I choose? I have at least one from every place I've lived."

The Bible tells us, though, that we do have many kindred spirits. If we are created in God's image, it stands to reason that God is our perfect bosom friend—and He goes with us wherever we go. It also stands to reason that if we are *all* created in God's image, we *all* have the potential to be kindred spirits with one another. At first glance, this sometimes seems impossible, but even Anne Shirley, as she encountered new and eccentric characters throughout her eight books, discovered that bosom friends could be found in even the most unexpected people.

Father, bring out Your Kindred Spirit in me that I may be a bosom friend to the people You bring my way. Open my heart to every possibility. I thank You, Lord! Amen.

My Thorn

"Therefore, in order to keep me from becoming conceited, I was given a thorn in my flesh, a messenger of Satan, to torment me. Three times I pleaded with the Lord to take it away from me. But he said to me, 'My grace is sufficient for you, for my power is made perfect in weakness.'"–2 Corinthians 12:7-9

I'm thankful that Paul felt led to write about his thorn in the flesh, whatever it was. I'm even more thankful he wrote about God's response when Paul asked God to take it away. The greatest missionary who ever lived had an on-going problem that tormented him, yet he saw it as a blessing because it forced him to rely on God.

Personally, I sometimes think moving qualifies as a thorn in the flesh. A needed sense of belonging takes a while to grow as I meet people and find my place in each new community. Even more time will pass before I gain enough confidence to let acquaintances see the real Janet normally hidden inside. When recently-established friends begin to express surprise at some of the things I say or comment on the mischief lying under the reserve, I know I'm relaxing and accepting a place as my own.

This increase in confidence is good, unless I'm tempted to take control. Control belongs to God. If I'm ever tempted to say, "Thanks for the help, Lord. I can take it from here. You can watch and cheer me on," I know I'm walking on dangerous ground. Paul rightly calls this attitude conceit. In order to be the person God wants me to be, I must rely on Him every moment of every day for every little thing.

And so, like Paul, I'm thankful for the thorn that forces me to lean on God. As I face the scary unknown, I can look to God and say,

"You take it from here and for always, Lord. I'll just watch and cheer you on." God's power is perfect in my weakness.

For Your sake, Lord, I delight in moving difficulties. "For when I am weak, then I am strong" (2 Corinthians 12:10). Amen.

Love and Faithfulness

"Let love and faithfulness never leave you; bind them around your neck, write them on the tablet of your heart. Then you will win favor and a good name in the sight of God and man."
–Proverbs 3:3-4

The key to winning favor and a good name is mysterious, yet simple. Favor from God and man, and the good reputation that comes with it, are things we desire for ourselves. Yet, according to King Solomon, you win these by giving of yourself to others, by showing love and being faithful.

Some people try to win friends and favor by telling others (and God) how wonderful they think they are. Unfortunately, this usually earns them the opposite response; people begin to avoid them, labeling them as braggarts and dreading yet another story of wit and accomplishment. Sadder still, these people are usually the loneliest, deep inside, with the lowest self-esteem of all. The tool they use to impress others, talking about themselves, only makes their situation worse.

The truth is clear: if you desire friendship and respect, you have to forget about yourself. Love others. Encourage their stories, and *listen* to learn what's important to them. Ask God to show you what you can do to bring a little more happiness into someone's life. Keep secrets. Refuse to start or spread gossip. Meet needs when you can, and pray continually when you can't. Rejoice in the success of others instead of jealously looking for success of your own. When you faithfully put the interests of others first, always showing God's love, you'll find life's elusive favor and a good name without even looking. God sees your actions and is pleased; you'll never go unnoticed when you live fully for Him.

Father, help me to bind love and faithfulness toward You and others around my neck. Tie the knot securely; then write these on the tablet of my heart as well. With these as my focus, I trust I'll find the acceptance I need. Thank You, Lord. Amen.

No Choice Needed

"But the Lord said to Samuel, 'Do not consider his appearance or his height, for I have rejected him. The Lord does not look at the things people look at. People look at the outward appearance, but the Lord looks at the heart.'" –1 Samuel 16:7

We often hear how important first impressions are, and we talk about the process of sizing one another up to see how we'll get along. But while I always try to make a good first impression on friends-to-be and hope they'll find me worthy of friendship, God has made it clear that we don't have to approach one another this way.

You see when I decide how I'll act toward someone based solely on a first, or even second or third, impression, I'm making my decision with extremely limited and, most likely, faulty information. If I size someone else up, I'm really considering whether or not that person is my equal. If my self-esteem is low, I may choose to defer to what seems to be a superior being—like Samuel was tempted to do upon seeing Jesse's oldest son in 1 Samuel 16. If I'm feeling especially good about myself, on the other hand, I may treat someone with less-than-deserved respect. It's only if I see another as an equal that friendship can form if I count on my first impressions.

God challenges me to choose friends in a different way, though. He sees their hearts; I trust Him to help me see them through His eyes. For this reason, I don't have to make up my mind whether or not I'm going to like someone right away. I'm simply to greet each new person God brings into my life as I would a cherished friend. If God reveals over time that this person is untrustworthy, then I can gently step away. As for first impressions, though, mine should always be,

"Thank You, Lord, for this new friend to love. I'll treat her well. Amen."

213

Whom to Please

"Am I now trying to win the approval of human beings, or of God? Or am I trying to please people? If I were still trying to please people, I would not be a servant of Christ." –Galatians 1:10

All people are born with a deep need for approval, acceptance, and affirmation. We want to know that we are loved and that we belong. Women who move frequently often find themselves working to have this need met. This can make them vulnerable to some temptations that "stationary" women would never consider.

Look at the contrast: people who live in the same community for a lifetime learn what those in the community expect. Without giving it much thought, they naturally adapt in order to fit in. So long as nothing happens to change their circumstances, they live happily ever after in the manner they have learned. Those who change communities frequently, however, may struggle to understand the rules of each new place in a desperate attempt to fit in.

What we have to remember, though, is that God never meant for us to fit in among the general population of the planet Earth. He gave us the need for approval, acceptance, and affirmation so we would seek it *in Him.* Once we realize this, we can embrace the moving process even as we struggle through it. Each move is a reminder that we can't rely on people or places or things to meet our deepest social needs. When our hearts long for acceptance, we are wise to turn to God.

Father, I choose to serve Christ wherever I go—whether people approve or not. I'll trust You to meet the needs You put in my heart. Amen.

Pleasing God First

"Whoever sows to please their flesh, from the flesh will reap destruction; whoever sows to please the Spirit, from the Spirit will reap eternal life." –Galatians 6:8

Of course, women aren't the only people looking for approval, acceptance, and affirmation. Our husbands and children seek it, too. Older children and teenagers are especially vulnerable. Peer pressure is a powerful tool in the hands of established cliques against the new kids in town. It's obvious that we parents have to teach our children to stay away from those things we automatically think of when we hear words like *teenager*, *peer pressure*, and *sin nature* in the same sentence. But pleasing the sin nature doesn't have to mean getting involved in drugs, violence, or premarital sex.

Pleasing the sin nature means letting anything take the place of God in our life. If making friends is more important than fellowship with God, even if those friends aren't pressuring us or our families into doing something blatantly wrong, we're still working to please the sin nature. When Matthew told us to "seek first his kingdom and his righteousness, and all these things will be given to you as well" (6:33), he had good reason. God has to come first if everything else is to fall into place, even friendships, as they should. Giving anything else top priority will result in destruction every time.

Lord, I want to please Your Spirit above all. Help my children to understand this that I may teach them to love You first as well. Amen.

Hearing

"So they took away the stone. Then Jesus looked up and said, 'Father, I thank you that you have heard me.'" –John 11:41

"You didn't hear what I said. Listen while I say it again."

Sometimes when we're talking, Mike will say these words to me. I want to listen to him; listening to understand expresses my love for him. Sometimes, however, my overeager brain rushes ahead, finishing Mike's thoughts for him in a seemingly logical way. That done I plan what should be a brilliant response before Mike even completes his statement. When my response doesn't match his words, though, he knows right away what I've done. I appreciate the correction and a second chance to listen to the one I truly love.

It's frustrating when someone we talk to misunderstands. When we realize the person failed to listen, it hurts. We're all subject to distraction at one time or another, but if we allow our minds to wander too often, we'll find we have few friends. People need to be heard.

On the other hand, if we discipline ourselves to listen consistently and make every attempt to understand, people will be drawn to that. Perhaps this is why Jesus made it clear that God hears. He *always* hears. It's a gift of love to you.

As you begin your life in this new town, talk to the Friend who listens all the time. Listen for His loving response and pray that He'll help you understand. Then listen to your spouse; you may begin to understand him in a way you couldn't before. Listen to your children. Really try to see what's in their hearts. Listen to your neighbors to seek peace and common ground. Listen—and you'll find new friends.

Father, You gave me two ears. Remind me to use them to show people they matter, to show them that I care. Thank You also for hearing me. I know You always do. Amen.

Looking for Barnabas

"But Barnabas took him and brought him to the apostles. He told them how Saul on his journey had seen the Lord and that the Lord had spoken to him, and how in Damascus he had preached fearlessly in the name of Jesus." –Acts 9:27

Finding acceptance in a new community can be challenging, especially if everyone there knows everyone else and follows a predictable, long-standing routine. Newcomers may find themselves treated with suspicion or distrust—sometimes, even disdain.

Shortly after his conversion, Paul tried to join the Christian community in Jerusalem. Not surprisingly, they weren't enthusiastic about having former persecutor, the persecutor-of-all-persecutors to be precise, in their midst. If it weren't for Barnabas, Paul probably would have had to set off on his own.

Just as God provided Barnabas to encourage and vouch for Paul, He can provide people to welcome and introduce us to others, as well. Pray that He will as you begin to seek out friends. One congenial Barnabas on your side can be the link to many happy relationships in your new town.

Father, I'm ready to make friends. Please open someone's heart to all You've given me to offer. Lead me to a kindhearted Barnabas of my own. Amen.

Eyes off Self

"I, even I, am he who comforts you. Who are you that you fear mere mortals, human beings, who are but grass?" –Isaiah 51:12

When I walk into a room full of people I've never met, I sometimes feel nervous, as if I'm surrounded by fearsome creatures. I fear rejection. I am afraid everyone will look down on me, and that I won't measure up to whatever standards I imagine they've set. I dread standing alone in the middle of the room, unnoticed, or worse yet, noticed, but ignored. At times like these, I start looking for a quiet chair in a dark corner with the intention of fading into the wallpaper until everyone goes home.

When I feel this way, however, my eyes are on myself. I've let my fears move me into a defensive stance. Seeking a hideout is a means of self-preservation. But what am I protecting myself from? Truthfully—from my own imagination.

A better approach is to focus on God before I enter that room, to ask Him for comfort—and guidance, too. I must realize that He created each person there and thank Him for the opportunity to meet someone new. Then I must remember that I'm Christ's servant; my task for the time being is to show others His love.

As I enter the room, I can greet people with a smile and a confident handshake. Then if I still feel like running for the wallpaper, I can look to see who's already there and reach out to make a new friend—or rescue the person standing in the middle of the room feeling unnoticed or ignored. (I understand how that person feels, after all.) If I take the time to look around instead of looking inside, I'll find there are lots of people fighting their own fears just as I am fighting mine. All we all need is acceptance and love.

Father, You created us all. Why do I fear? Help me to meet needs instead as I receive (and give) comfort from You. Amen.

A Fair Appraisal

"Do not judge, or you too will be judged. For in the same way you judge others, you will be judged, and with the measure you use, it will be measured to you." –Matthew 7:1-2

I used to see this passage as a threat: "If you judge others, God's gonna judge *you!*" But God's gonna judge *everyone* someday, regardless of how we've treated others, and His judgment will be fair. Naturally, how we've appraised others will be reflected in God's judgment, but I think Jesus' words go beyond this point. I think Jesus was giving us some very practical advice on getting along with each other.

When our family first began attending services in one new locale, a certain woman stood out as bubbly, friendly, and loved by all. But week after week, she was standoffish toward me. She didn't talk to me except to nod her head in passing. Sometimes I wondered if she intentionally walked around the place where I stood in order to avoid contact with me. I couldn't figure out what I could have done to offend her and began to think of her as a snob. My feelings were hurt, and I began to avoid her as much as I imagined she was avoiding me.

Then God helped me to see this woman from another point of view. He showed me that I'm talkative and friendly around people I know and trust, but tend to avoid first contact with strangers. I began to wonder if this woman was the same way. To test the theory, I decided to make an effort to communicate more.

I quickly discovered that this woman was friendly and eager to talk whenever I approached her. She didn't seem distant. There was no chip on her shoulder toward me. I truly imagined it all, allowing a wall to rise between us in the process. With God's eyes, though, I found a new friend in an apparent foe.

Father, teach me to leave the judging to You. With Your superhuman help, I can overcome fear to reach those who seem unreachable. Help me show Your love equally to all. Amen.

Chapter 12
Finding Your Niche

What to Do?

"Trust in the Lord and do good; dwell in the land and enjoy safe pasture." –Psalm 37:3

Moving is such a frantic time. Pack boxes. Clean the old place. Clean the new place. Unpack boxes. Hurry, hurry, hurry! There's so much to do—then suddenly, there's nothing to do. My husband goes to work. Our children go to school. I find myself home alone with no commitments, no close friends. This is when panic sets in.

"What should I do?" I ask. Should I volunteer to teach a class at church? Help out at the kids' school? Maybe one of the organizations on post needs me? I want to make a good impression on everyone, of course. Getting involved and over-involved may accomplish this. So many options, yet no commitments yet—so still nothing to do.

There is something to do, though. This is the time to "trust in the Lord" and pray. When you reach this point in your transition, take. your. time. Ask God what He has planned for you to do in this new place, and wait for His answer in *His* time.

Next, "do good." Look for little ways to make a difference. Bake cookies for the school bake sale and casseroles for the church potluck. Smile. Invite a new friend out to lunch.

Finally, "dwell in the land and enjoy safe pasture." Before you commit, dwell. *Live* in your new home and enjoy what it has to offer. Explore your new community. Don't be afraid; claim it as your own safe place. In time you'll have more than enough to do. For now, talk to God and savor time in your new home.

Lord, I'm tempted to jump at every opportunity that comes my way. Help me to choose wisely based on guidance from You. While I wait, I choose to focus on You in the comfort of this new home. Thank You for this time and this place. Amen.

Being Mary

"Mary has chosen what is better, and it will not be taken away from her." –Luke 10:42

Over the years, I've discovered that when it comes to Luke 10:38-42, most women relate better to Martha than to Mary. We're busy, busy, busy—and, sometimes, we resent anyone who isn't. At risk of being stoned, however, let me share something I've discovered through move after move. I enjoy life more, find it more fulfilling, and accomplish more worthwhile things when I follow Mary's example instead of Martha's. Jesus knew what He was talking about.

The school in the Netherlands was quite a bit further from home than the school my boys had attended in New York. Instead of scooting around the corner ten minutes before class, they met the bus 40 minutes before school. Suddenly I had almost two extra hours of time home alone! To add to this time when the school year first started, I had no commitments. We hadn't lived there long enough for me get involved.

Rather than count the minutes until my precious children returned safely home, I decided to catch up on my reading. I discovered several books on prayer, solitude, and practicing God's presence. Then I let God teach me how to put some of the things they taught into practice. I began to relate to Mary sitting at Jesus' feet instead of Martha in the kitchen.

The best was yet to come, though. As I spent time with Jesus, He began to say to me *exactly* what Martha had told Him to say to Mary. He showed me tasks to complete, stories to write, and people to reach out to for Him. I learned which commitments were important in His eyes, and that gave them value in mine. Slowly, I became busy again, but I'm still sitting at Jesus' feet.

Jesus, I need Your presence. I need Your wisdom. I want to soak it all in. As I go about my business, remind me to spend every moment with You. Amen.

The Importance of Purpose

"And David knew that the Lord had established him as king over Israel and that his kingdom had been highly exalted for the sake of his people Israel." –1 Chronicles 14:2

David knew that God had chosen him to lead God's people. He knew his purpose, and it gave his role meaning. I'm sure there were times when the quiet life of a harp-playing shepherd on the hills sounded good to him. But God called him somewhere else, and, most of the time, David enthusiastically worked to fulfill that calling.

Likewise, the one thing that helps me feel most settled in a place is finding my specific purpose there. Before I arrive, I begin to pray that God will show me what to do and help me to do it well. Sometimes I find a meaningful-made-for-Janet task right away. Other times, I've left a place wondering if God used me at all, but trusting that He did. In either case, I've learned to seek and pray and trust God has a purpose for me.

Finding purpose in our move to the Netherlands proved to be a matter of timing. I'd been there only a few weeks when a new friend in the chapel offered a teaching position to me. I almost grabbed it without hesitation but felt the need to wait and pray. I did so for several days, anxious to give my answer, but finding no go-ahead. Finally in exasperation, I prayed, "Lord, don't you want me to teach this class?"

Surprisingly His answer was, "No." I was amazed to learn that God had assigned that class to someone else, someone who spoke up quickly after I turned it down. A few months later, one of the chapel pianists moved to her new home. A new one was needed, and I was available. I knew this was the task for me.

Father, I know Your purpose for me is perfect. Please use me in Your time, with Your wisdom, and with or without my knowledge. Until You reveal Your role for me, I will trust and pray. Amen.

Not a Transplant

***"For just as each of us has one body with many members, and
these members do not all have the same function, so in Christ we,
though many, form one body, and each member belongs to all the
others."* –Romans 12:4-5**

As I move from place to place, I often think of myself as being
transplanted. If I'm comparing myself to a flower or tree being uprooted
from one place and planted again somewhere else, the analogy works.
But as I think about the body of Christ, I realize this term, transplant,
doesn't fit at all. There is only *one* body of Christ, therefore I can't
possibly be a liver or a heart or a kidney surgically removed from one
body and placed in another. I am a member of the body of Christ
wherever I go. I have a function to perform; I belong.

Since I circulate, maybe that makes me a red blood cell. I travel
around the body carrying nutrients where they're most needed. I like that
picture: somehow it gives moving purpose. And as I look back over my
roles in different churches throughout the years, I can see that God has
often used me to fill holes others have left or to provide temporary relief
for someone who's worked hard and needs time to soak up some fresh
spiritual strength. Christ's body needs red blood cells as much as it needs
shoulders and knees and pinky toes.

I find it comforting to know that whether I function as a red
blood cell, bone marrow, or a strand of hair, I can walk confidently into
any Christian church and know that I belong. I can then ask God to help
me function according to His perfect design. Rejection isn't even a
concern; I'm not a transplant. Christ's body is alive all over the globe,
and I am a part with purpose.

*Thank You for receiving me as a healthy member of your body, Lord. Let
me never forget: thanks to You, I belong. Amen.*

A God-Shaped Life

"Do not conform to the pattern of this world, but be transformed by the renewing of your mind. Then you will be able to test and approve what God's will is—his good, pleasing and perfect will."
–Romans 12:2

When my husband took his first pastorate, I wanted to be the perfect, little, pastor's wife—to discover and meet everyone's expectations of me. Fortunately, our church gave me a copy of H. B. London and Neil B. Wiseman's book, *Married to a Pastor's Wife*. After reading it, I realized there's no such thing as the perfect, little, pastor's wife. All pastors' wives are different; I just had to be me.

The same has proved true since I've become a chaplain's wife (same husband, new ministry). All chaplains' spouses are different, and expectations for them seem to change with each assignment, too. Fitting into the mold will never be possible for me.

If I go through life letting my environment determine who I am, what I'm interested in, and how I will spend my time, my personality will have to change with every move. This isn't what God has in mind for me. Instead of conforming to the world as I may be tempted to do, I have to let God renew my mind. I have to let Him reveal His will for my life. I have to let Him shape me into the person He means for me to be.

As God does this for me, I can move more confidently from place to place choosing friends and activities with the conviction of who I am and whose. Instead of forcing myself into one uncomfortable mold after another, I'm free to impact my environment for God in the way that He has planned—for His glory and for everyone's good.

Divine Master, shape my life as You will. Please make it strong, so no one but You can change its shape. I leave myself in Your capable hands. I'm forever Yours! Amen.

229

Old Spices

"You are the salt of the earth. But if the salt loses its saltiness, how can it be made salty again? It is no longer good for anything, except to be thrown out and trampled underfoot." –Matthew 5:13

A funny thing happens whenever I've been in a new house for a while. One day, I'll decide to boldly try a new recipe that actually involves cooking with original ingredients—from scratch, what a concept! (My family warms up the car for a pizza run whenever I do this, just in case.) As I reach for spices buried in the back of my cupboard and covered with dust, I notice labels from stores that aren't available at my current locale. Usually, I can trace the spice to a store from our previous city, but sometimes I have to go back even farther than that. Time to clean out the cupboards. My cooking's bad enough without spices that have lost their zing.

Just as I clean out my cupboard to rid it of things that may ruin my already challenged cooking, I must let God clean out my life from time to time. As I sit quietly before Him with an open heart, He removes grudges, misjudgments, sour attitudes, and anything else that keeps me from being an effective member of His kingdom. Did you catch that? My job is to sit quietly before Him *with an open heart*. His job is to preserve the salt of my life. My cupboard doesn't protest when I pull aging spices out. In fact, if it could be thankful, it probably would. I must be thankful when God does the same for me.

Keep the salt fresh, Lord. Make me effective for You. Amen.

Established Work

"May the favor of the Lord our God rest on us; establish the work of our hands for us—yes, establish the work of our hands."
–Psalm 90:17

To establish something is to set it up permanently. Yet moving often makes most of life's activities very temporary. So how does Psalm 90:17 apply to the woman who moves?

Before I married, I felt called to the ministry. I still do. As I pursued ordination, though, I ran into a snag. Completing my education was easy. But being ordained required three years of service on a local church staff. As I prayed about that aspect of the ministry, God showed me that I'd never be able to establish myself in a local church ministry in a practical way. I realized that about the time I'd find a place to serve in any new home, Mike would receive orders and we'd move somewhere else. I knew this would prove heartbreaking, if not frustrating, to me, and would be unfair to any church I'd serve. Further, as I reflected on what ordination would mean, I found a little statement in our denomination's materials that helped me understand that ordination is meant for those called to *lead* or *administrate*. My calling is to teach and to write. As it turns out, these activities fit well into my transient life.

Wherever we go, there are classes to teach. Further, I can teach the ones I feel strongest about over and over again to new groups of people in each location. Writing is something I can do anywhere. My work continues with little or no interruption as we move from place to place, and my experiences all over add flavor to whatever I write.

Other friends have discovered their own occupations and hobbies that travel well, too. Some teach or substitute-teach in Department of Defense schools. Some quilt, sew, or do other crafty things. One even volunteers in post thrift shops and usually works herself into a full or part-time job before each move. Meaningful work, for enjoyment or for pay, gives a touch of stability to a life in flux.

Establish the work of our hands, dear Lord, and we will know we're blessed. Amen.

Forgetting

"But one thing I do: Forgetting what is behind and straining
toward what is ahead, I press on toward the goal to win the prize
for which God has called me heavenward in Christ Jesus."
–Philippians 3:13-14

The meaning of this verse becomes vivid to me just after a move. The line is suddenly black and white: forget what you left at your old place; get on with this new life. Of course, Paul wasn't talking about an old residence. He was talking about an old way of life. Take a look at verses four through six of this chapter. Paul was forgetting his confidence in his own good works to make him good inside. Paul was forgetting his letter-of-the-law perfect pedigree. Paul was forgetting the way he persecuted Christ's own people in order to further his own glorious career.

When I look at all Paul forgot in order to go on with his new life in Christ, I realize that God doesn't want me to forget *everything* I leave behind when I move. Family, friends, and good memories are precious. We're to treasure them as gifts from God even after we move away from them. What we are to forget is bad habits, fear, hurt feelings, negative attitudes, sin. When you pack your boxes, leave these things behind. As you decorate your new home, replace these things with prayer, time in God's Word, and new friends who will help you press on toward Heaven. This physical move from one location to another is the perfect opportunity for a spiritual move toward Heaven, too.

Father in Heaven, if I've brought anything to this new home that keeps me from pressing on toward You, help me to forget it now. Show me what You've provided in this new place to help me move closer to You. Amen.

Johnny Appleseed

"Therefore go and make disciples of all nations, baptizing them in the name of the Father and of the Son and of the Holy Spirit."
–Matthew 28:19

The last words of Matthew contain a passage known as "The Great Commission." These were Jesus' last words to His disciples before His departure to Heaven. "Go make disciples," He said. "Teach them to obey everything I've commanded you" (from verse 20).

In Acts 1:8, He says, "and you will be my witnesses in Jerusalem, and in all Judea and Samaria, and to the ends of the earth." His disciples had come through three years of intense training. Now it was their turn to teach.

As Christians, the commission is ours as well. First we learn and observe the truth from those who learned before us; then we pass it on to those who are waiting to hear. Those of us who move frequently can fulfill this commission in a unique way. We may not be in one place long enough to nurture and disciple as much as we'd like, but we can move from place to place with a Johnny Appleseed mentality.

Just as Johnny traveled about the country planting trees that he never saw grow, we can plant seeds of God's love, spreading the Gospel wherever we go. We can even water those seeds some with the use of social media, the telephone, and even letters, encouraging the seedlings from our past to get or stay involved in church with local contacts who can help them grow.

Teacher, as I go to "the ends of the earth," help me to be your witness. Use me to make new disciples wherever I go. Amen.

Something Bigger

"Lift up your eyes to the heavens, look at the earth beneath; the heavens will vanish like smoke, the earth will wear out like a garment and its inhabitants die like flies. But my salvation will last forever, my righteousness will never fail" –Isaiah 51:6

When our family visited England a few years ago, we spent an afternoon in Epworth, the birthplace of John and Charles Wesley. One of the historical sites in this quiet town is the final resting place of the Wesley brothers' father, Samuel. When leaders of the church that John grew up in, his father's former church, refused to let John preach within its walls, John stood on his father's tomb outside the church and spoke to the crowd from that perch.

A few weeks after that trip, I was practicing piano for an upcoming offertory. My choice was "The Church's One Foundation." As I was turning a page, I happened to catch the composer's name: Samuel Wesley. I doubt he ever imagined that an Army chaplain's wife raising three boys would be playing his music in a military chapel two hundred and fifty years after he wrote it! Suddenly I was part of something bigger than myself. Samuel Wesley wrote the music; Samuel Stone wrote the words. Two and a half centuries later, God is still seeking people to carry the message, "The Church's one foundation is Jesus Christ, her Lord." Come to think of it, that message began its journey long before Samuel Wesley lay in his grave. In his first letter to the Corinthians, Paul wrote, "For no one can lay any foundation other than the one already laid, which is Jesus Christ" (3:11). I have no doubt that God will lead someone else to deliver the message long after I'm in my heavenly home.

From this perspective, the trials of moving seem less significant. Two and half centuries from now, they won't matter at all. Yet those efforts that build God's kingdom are labors that will last.

Father, lift my eyes from this earth to Your kingdom. Show me how to build on Christ, my Lord. Amen.

Chapter 13
Accepting Your Home

Christ: The Constant

"We are confident, I say, and would prefer to be away from the body and at home with the Lord. So we make it our goal to please him, whether we are at home in the body or away from it."
–2 Corinthians 5:8-9

I don't think the apostle Paul ever felt at home while living "in the body," in other words, alive on Planet Earth. "Home" for Paul was with the Lord, and he taught that this should be true for *all* of God's children. As we live out our God-given days in this world, we can train ourselves to set our minds on spending eternity with the Father of All.

Still, those of us who move around often long for even a temporary sense of "home," the feeling that we belong, are loved, participate, and are secure in our surroundings. Paul must have recognized this need, for he gives us the key to finding just that in 2 Corinthians 5:9: "We make it our goal to please [Christ]."

If our sole desire is to serve Christ, to honor Him in everything we say and do, then, and only then, will we feel "at home in the body." Amazingly enough, once we know we're living in the center of God's will, truly serving and pleasing Him, we'll find that "at home" feeling wherever we go. I guess you could say that as we strive to make Christ feel at home in our hearts (welcome, loved, and in charge of the action), He turns anyplace with Him into our home away from Home.

Jesus, I love you! Welcome to my heart—my life is Yours. With You, I'm always home. Amen.

Angry Puzzle Pieces

"But in fact God has placed the parts in the body, every one of them, just as he wanted them to be." –1 Corinthians 12:18

Imagine working a complicated jigsaw puzzle. You finally find the piece to fill a nagging hole and triumphantly put it in place. Then something strange happens. The piece speaks to you and says, "I don't want to be here. Put me somewhere else."

Then the other placed pieces join in, complaining about their spots, and the yet-to-be-placed pieces demand to be placed right away. If you listen to the angry puzzle pieces, you'll never reach your goal: a complete and beautiful picture.

Likewise, God has a plan, a glorious objective in which each of us has a part. If we are living in submission to His will, we are right where He wants us to be—even if we're not where we think we want to be.

Living overseas, for example, was challenging to me. I often prayed, "But Lord, I'm an American. I don't think I belong over here. Are You sure You meant to put me in this place?"

Then God assured me, in one way or another, that I was right where He wanted me then.

God doesn't mind when I ask for reassurance; I'm His child. As my loving, heavenly Father, He's happy to give that to me. He only minds when I complain. My place in this world is His choice.

Master Puzzle Maker, I am just one puzzle piece. Place me where You want me to be. Please make Your picture complete. Amen.

Meek Movers

"Blessed are the meek, for they will inherit the earth."
–Matthew 5:5

Here's a new way to look at this verse: *Blessed are those movers who humbly submit to God's will for their lives, for they will fill their heads with happy memories of planting their footprints all over the globe.*

Wait! Before you slam this book shut, shouting, "Jesus didn't say that!" please hear me out. You see, way back in the beginning, God gave the earth and everything in it to Adam and Eve. But they messed up, and in doing so, allowed the world to be ruled by sin. Jesus triumphantly took it back when He died on the cross and was raised to life again, and He graciously gives it to those who faithfully follow Him. Therefore, the meek will inherit the earth.

Now if we find ourselves moving from place to place about the globe and recognize that this is God's will for our lives, we can choose to meekly accept God's will or fight it. Those who fight it either find themselves living somewhere other than where God wants them or grumbling about their unhappy lot in life. Personally, I don't care for either option.

However, those who submit will find themselves blessed with contentment. No, I didn't say their lives would be perfect and that nothing would ever go wrong. I said they would find themselves blessed with contentment. As God leads them from place to place, they'll have peace in their souls and happy memories of walking with God all over the world. In a sense, God gives us each place we live as our own. We may not have the deed yet, but we have the knowledge and the memories. The meek will inherit the earth; we movers just get a head start.

I'm walking with You all over the world, Lord. And as You lead, I claim each place as home. Amen.

Home at Last

"You will go out in joy and be led forth in peace; the mountains and hills will burst into song before you, and all the trees of the field will clap their hands." –Isaiah 55:12

Have you felt it yet? I just did! We've lived here nearly a year, and as I drove around the city it suddenly felt *right*. My heart has finally claimed this place as home. I know I am where I belong.

It's not a perfect home; such a place does not exist on Earth. But for now, it's mine. I understand it. I function well within it. When I leave, I will miss it. I'm making memories with my family here, finding favorite places to eat and shop and play, and enjoying my spot on this planet for this time of my life.

As I go out into the community, I experience the joy and peace of the familiar. I delight in landscapes I've come to know. They no longer dare me risk entrance. They welcome me as a friend. The forbidden strangeness is gone—I've been accepted and have accepted in return.

This is the goal when we move. It takes time—months, sometimes more. With prayer, determination, and an openness to God's will, you'll find this promised peace and joy. You'll find yourself at home.

Thank You, Lord, for enabling me to go out with peace and joy again. Amen.

Enjoying Now

"Do not say, 'Why were the old days better than these?' For it is not wise to ask such questions." –Ecclesiastes 7:10

When we lived in Kansas City, we discovered a restaurant called, *Tippin's*. We *loved* this restaurant! I ordered the same thing almost every time: hot cream of broccoli and cheese soup with homemade cornbread on the side with the best honey butter I've ever tasted. Sometimes I substituted half a turkey sandwich for the cornbread, but whichever I chose, the meal was always delicious. My mouth still waters when I think about it.

When we lived in the Netherlands, I had to stop thinking about it. Dutch people don't eat out quite as often as American people do. There was no *Tippin's* in the Netherlands—or anything like it for that matter—unless it came out of my own kitchen—which kind of defeats the point. Don't you think?

If I thought about *Tippin's* in the Netherlands, my thoughts were like King Solomon's, "Oh, why were the old days better than these?" But they weren't better, just different, and I had to remember that—always!

When I think of Kansas City, I remember *Tippin's* with fondness. But the Netherlands, and every other place I've lived, has had its own good things for our family to eat. In the Netherlands, for example, we enjoyed pannekoeken, stroopwafels, and broodjes. Those are treats we'll never find, authentically, in Kansas City.

Heavenly Father, thank You for the delightful taste of now. I'm eating it up. Amen.

Tuning the Piano

"Whatever your hand finds to do, do it with all your might."
–Ecclesiastes 9:10

For my first Christmas after my wedding, my parents wrapped a homemade coupon good for a free piano tuning. Mike and I expected to move within months, so we decided to wait to use the coupon. (Pianos need tuning every time you move them.) Our circumstances changed, however, and we stayed in San Diego an extra year. Once we did move, it was to a temporary apartment. Always anticipating yet another move, we ignored the piano's need.

It was after the birth of our third son that my mom finally put her foot down. Pulling out the yellow pages, she said, "You're having that piano tuned during *this* visit. No more excuses!" She hired a tuner, who was shocked at the neglected condition of my poor piano. But he fixed it anyway, and we enjoyed the fresh sound—until we moved again.

Moving gives us an excuse to put things off. For example:

—We need a new dining room table, but if we buy it now, it might get scratched when we move next year.

—I'd be good at that job, but would taking it for less than a year be fair?

—I never resolved that argument, but we're moving away. It doesn't matter now.

If you *need* something, buy it. You may always be moving, so if you don't buy what you need, you'll always do without.

Pursue your interests and use your talents. So long as people know up front how long you expect to stay, you are treating them fairly.

Always strive to make peace. If you move without trying, you'll carry the memory of the hurt to your new home. You don't need that extra baggage. Do your best to lighten the load.

Father, when my hands find something to do, help me to put excuses aside. I'll do the task with all my might. I'll tune that piano today. Amen.

How to Take the Land

"Now, Israel, hear the decrees and laws I am about to teach you. Follow them so that you may live and may go in and take possession of the land the Lord, the God of your ancestors, is giving you." –Deuteronomy 4:1

When the Israelites entered Canaan, their goal was a complete takeover. They were to completely destroy or forever run out of town the people occupying their God-given land. Needless to say, this is not our goal when we move to a new place. Our goal is to make our home *among* the people in our new community. Once we feel an inner sense of belonging or rightness about a place, we've "taken possession." We've reached our goal.

Deuteronomy 4 tells us how to do this: Follow God's law. Summed up, the Ten Commandments, found in Deuteronomy 5, tell us how to get along with God and with others. Once we've learned to do this, we can make friends—godly friends—just about anywhere. There's nothing like a Christian friend to help one feel at home.

Think about it: If God is number one in your life and everything you do is for His glory, your actions and choices will reflect that priority. Your true friends will be Christians who also want to honor God. (You'll find them in the Bible-believing church you choose to attend regularly.) Non-believing neighbors and acquaintances will see the positive way you relate to God and to one another and will be drawn by God's Spirit to want to learn more. Suddenly you'll have new brothers and sisters in Christ, and you'll have "taken possession" of the land. I make it sound simple, but it requires a complete focus on God and obedience to His Word. Live for Him, and He'll help you make a home—anywhere.

Master, teach me Your law. Help me obey. Show me how to take this land for You. Amen.

My Earthquake

"Therefore we will not fear, though the earth give way and the mountains fall into the heart of the sea." –Psalm 46:2

Growing up in Southern California, I developed a healthy respect for earthquakes. When I feel one starting up, I know what to do, where to go. The response is automatic and deliberate: move slowly to the nearest doorframe, brace yourself, and hang on. Of course, most Southern California earthquakes are over before anyone can get anywhere near a doorframe (or under a heavy desk), but at least I know what to do. And when the quick-kind-of-quake is over, the kind where _no one_ is hurt, one word always comes to mind: Cool! Mild earthquakes give me the same thrill as a roller coaster ride. Just think: a surprise adrenaline rush straight from our awesome, creator God!

That's why I was so amazed and excited one early morning in the Netherlands when an earthquake, the first there in ten years, shook our house while I was reading upstairs. Our family has spent a lot of time in Southern California, but my boys had to move to the Netherlands to feel their first earthquake! Two out of three thought their daddy was playing a trick on them while they slept in their beds; all were woken up. You could say that day began with quite a jolt.

Comparing the quake to others I've experienced, I guessed it to be about 4.8. When the news reported 4.9, I felt I'd proved I'm still a Californian at heart. No one was hurt. A few castles were damaged. People weren't overly shaken up, so to speak. But the earthquake made my day: a gift from God to help me feel at home while far away.

Father, thank You for surprising me with reminders of home, in whatever form they come. You fill my heart with joy. Amen.

Following the Cloud

"In all the travels of the Israelites, whenever the cloud lifted from above the tabernacle, they would set out; but if the cloud did not lift, they did not set out—until the day it lifted." –Exodus 40:36-37

Sometimes I feel like an Israelite, wandering in seemingly aimless circles around the world, hoping to find the Promised Land. When facing a move, I wonder if our next stop will be that perfect land and, if it is, if we'll somehow get to stay. When settling into a new home, I look for the milk and honey. When the inevitable "droughts" come along, I realize I'm still on life's journey and remember I must trust God to help me face each challenge. Sometimes I'm tempted to look back—just like the Israelites did. Other times, I begin to look forward, wondering what our next home will be like and dreaming of the Promised Land.

In the best of times, however, I go about my daily business—just like the Israelites did. I look for reminders of God's presence, like the Israelites' looked for the cloud above the tabernacle. I've never seen a fiery cloud, but when I quietly look and listen I usually find something that reminds me God is there. Once assured, I can set out to do the tasks He has given for that day: loving and caring for my family, completing household chores, reading, writing, praying, and playing. Until the "cloud" lifts, I'm free to enjoy life wherever it is I am.

Ever-present Father, thank You for assurance that You're here. Help me to go about my business, enjoying this place until You say it's time to move on. Amen.

Character and Hope

"Not only so, but we also glory in our sufferings, because we know that suffering produces perseverance; perseverance, character; and character, hope." –Romans 5:3-4

"I don't know what's wrong with me," said a friend as a group of us visited one evening. "Lately, I've been frantic to sort and clean every room in my house—and I'm not even planning to move! Last week, I even cleaned out the garage. My husband thinks I'm going nuts."

"When did you move here?" asked another friend.

"We arrived three years ago."

She looked a little confused when we all started to smile and laugh, but she'd just solved her own mystery. She'd moved at least every three years for as long as she'd been an adult. Something inside her was programmed to begin the process whether she needed to or not.

Though laughing, we all felt sympathetic about our friend's "nesting" habits. We knew we'd probably be doing the same thing in her situation. Though we dread starting over, we've persevered through enough moves to know we can successfully handle another. Our transient lifestyles have become a part of our character, and though there are hurts and disappointments, we've learned to delight in many aspects of the process, too. There's something refreshing about cleaning out junk, packing up essentials, and starting anew. There's something exciting about going where you've never been before. Best of all, there's hope of new blessings, like interesting friends and meaningful opportunities.

When we faithfully persevere through the trials that come our way, God's Spirit uses them to build our character, a character that allows us to have hope in Him in any situation—even suddenly not having to move.

Holy Spirit, continue to do Your work in me through every situation. Amen.

Seeing the Fruit

"No longer will they build houses and others live in them, or plant and others eat. For as the days of a tree, so will be the days of my people; my chosen ones will long enjoy the work of their hands."
–Isaiah 65:22

My favorite thing about springtime in a new home is watching to see what flowers will come up. I grew up in Southern California where the flowers remain about the same all year long. I was surprised when a variety of Tulips and Daffodils appeared around our first little house in Kansas City. We didn't plant them, but there they were—and I loved them! In Maine, a tree produced crab apples. In New York, we found Peonies along with more Daffodils and Tulips. In the Netherlands, we got every kind of flower we know and more!

But we didn't plant them. Someone who planned to enjoy these natural treasures moved away and left them for us. In the same way, we've made improvements to each home we've enjoyed only to leave our handiwork for someone else's benefit. This seems kind of sad, but change is a fact of life. And I'm happy for those who are enjoying our projects as I enjoy flowers planted by those who came before me.

Someday, however, God promises we'll get to stay put. We'll enjoy the works of our hands and share by choice rather than circumstance. God has great plans for His people; I'm thankful to be a part.

Master, I'm looking forward to joining Your perfect community in the sky. What a pleasant dream! Until then, let me happily build to benefit others and thankfully enjoy surprises left behind for me. Amen.

Through Someone Else's Eyes

"I will give thanks to the Lord because of his righteousness; I will sing the praises of the name of the Lord Most High." –Psalm 7:17

Yesterday I took my parents to the airport after a three-week visit. We had such a good time. Of course, we had fun just being together, playing games, talking, catching up on all the news about changes in our lives. But I also enjoyed taking them out to explore my adopted world. Naturally, I took them to some places I'd never seen, expanding my borders of comfort in the process and finding adventure with my folks. My favorite times, though, were taking them to see the people and places I appreciate most.

This is what I discovered through those experiences: If my parents appreciated something I enjoy about this place, I was delighted and enjoyed the place even more. If they were disappointed, though, I actually became a little defensive: "You would love this place on a bright, sunny day. Too bad the weather is so bad."

Upon reflection, I see that this community is growing on me. I've made it my home, and I want the people I love to love it as I'm beginning to. It took seeing the world through someone else's eyes to help me realize this, but now that I have, I find I'm more content in this new home. For that I thank the Lord. He was right to bring me here. I knew that before, but I *see* it now. I'll continue to praise His good name.

Thank You, righteous Lord. You are good. You are wise. You are in control. You deserve all honor and praise, forever. I'll give all I can to You. Amen.

Enough Light

"Your word is a lamp for my feet, a light on my path."
–Psalm 119:105

When our family goes camping, one of our favorite activities is taking moonlight hikes around the campground. In the evening, you can see the night sky like you can't in the city, black and full of countless stars. You can hear (and sometimes see) nocturnal animals as they begin to forage for food. Our flashlights and lanterns don't let us see as much as we can by the light of day, but they let us see enough. They show us the path. So long as we stay on that path, we'll find the way back to our site.

Living in Europe, there were times when I would pray, "Lord, I'd really like to go home soon." Home in this case was anywhere in America. "I miss my country of birth, Lord," I'd continue, "I'm looking forward to heading back soon."

Once, though, as I prayed this homesickness prayer, God seemed to answer, "What if I want you to stay here another few years?" I had to think (and pray) about that.

My conclusion: I don't know what the future holds. God hasn't given me the light to see that far ahead. As I read His Word and pray, though, I know I'm on the right path and that is where I'll stay.

Guiding Light, thank You for Your Word that shows the way. I'll follow where it leads. Amen.

Creation Everywhere

"The earth is the Lord's, and everything in it, the world, and all who live in it." –Psalm 24:1

I've heard it said that Heaven will be ever so much more wonderful than anything we can see or imagine while here on Earth. If this is so, and I believe it is, then each move gives me more to anticipate.

Growing up in Southern California, I enjoyed the sunshine on my face, the smell of salt in the air, and the vast ocean—so big, it's hard to imagine God's bigger! In Kansas City, I witnessed the changing of the seasons for the first time. In Maine, I enjoyed ocean air from another coast, roads that wound around forests and lakes and more forests and lakes, and autumn leaves in colors I never imagined finding on trees. In New York, I experienced the extremes of winter—ice storms, beautiful, but deadly, and smooth blankets of fresh, white snow that gently wrapped our home up to the windowsills.

Later, in the Netherlands, I discovered an incredible new world of vegetation in bloom. Each year we visited Keukenhof, a museum of living flowers only open eight weeks a year. I never dreamed there were so many kinds of flowers! One whole pavilion was dedicated exclusively to varieties of orchid. Some of the tulips were almost as tall as my youngest son, with petals bigger than my hand. And there were surely more colors represented than are found in the biggest crayon box.

Experiencing nature's wonders all over the globe points my mind heavenward. I praise God for the creation He's given us to enjoy now and eagerly look forward to what's in store in our future forever home.

Thank You, Master Creator, for the wonders of this Earth and all that's yet to come. I am privileged to live where I can experience so much of it. Help me always to recognize Your signature in all You've made. Amen.

Laughter

"She is clothed in strength and dignity; she can laugh at the days to come." –Proverbs 31:25

We had only been living in the Netherlands for nine months when terms like *RFO* (Request For Orders) and *next assignment* began to creep into my husband's vocabulary. It seemed a little early, but each assignment only lasts about three years and plans for the next assignment must be set in motion far in advance—sometimes before we've even settled into the current one.

It seems we're always dreaming, making plans, changing plans, filling out paperwork (actually, that's Mike's part), and starting all over again. And we never really know where we're going next until we actually get there because military personnel needs change as circumstances around the world change, rapidly and unexpectedly.

This means I have a choice. I can worry and fret and pace and live in a state of general frustration. Or I can wrap my arms around life's roller coaster safety bar, hang on tight, and laugh at the crazy days to come. We never know where we're going next, though we may have a general idea. The military doesn't know where we're going next, though they are making plans. But God knows where we're going next—no doubt about it; there's nothing unexpected from His point of view. He sees the roller coaster from above, all the sudden twists, turns, ups and downs, and He knows where we'll end up.

Omniscient God, help me to face the future with strength, dignity, and laughter as I trust in You. Amen.

Moving In for the Last Time

"My Father's house has many rooms; if that were not so, would I have told you that I am going there to prepare a place for you?"
–John 14:2

As I quickly read through John 14:2, I get tired just thinking about it. Many rooms! That means many boxes! How will we ever settle in? Then I read the verse before and go on to the next. Jesus assures me everything will be all right.

In John 14:1, Jesus commands us to not let our hearts be troubled. We are to trust God. We are to trust His Son. We are to relax. No worries. God has everything under control.

In John 14:3, Jesus tells us that if He is going to His Father's house to prepare a place for us, then He will come back to take us there. No packing or unpacking. No cleaning. No travel arrangements. Jesus is taking care of everything.

Moving into Heaven will be better than moving into a pre-furnished house. Jesus knows our hearts, so the color scheme will be just right. In fact, it will be more beautiful than anything we can imagine. We won't have any suitcases to unpack; everything we need will already be there, made to fit just right. The view from our windows will be "to die for"—except that we will never die! That is the best part of all: eternal life in the presence of our loving, heavenly Father in a permanent home of which we'll never tire. Safe. Secure. Content. Joyful. Forever.

I don't know about you, but suddenly, I'm not tired anymore. For now I'll do my best with this home here on Earth. But someday I'll live in my heavenly Father's home, in the room prepared by Jesus just for me.

Jesus, thank You for promising Heaven someday. Amen.

A Home for God's Child

"Truly I tell you, anyone who will not receive the kingdom of God like a little child will never enter it." —Mark **10:15** and Luke **18:17** (See also Matthew 18:3.)

When grown-ups move from one home to another, their children move with them. They don't get a vote. They may not understand why. They may not even like or want the change. When their parents move, however, children move, too, because for children, home is where their parents are.

If we are the children of God, therefore, and He is our Father, home for us is where He Is. Since God is everywhere, in a broad sense, that could mean that home is anywhere. But anywhere doesn't bring up images of the comfort and security and context of home. No. In more personal terms, I think home for us is where God sends us, where God wants us, where God takes us, wherever God leads.

Jesus, God's Son, was sent to Earth by the Father. Our world became His home. Then He was taken back up to Heaven, His eternal home. And there, He is creating an eternal home for us.

For now, however, just like it was for Jesus, Earth is our home. We are God's children. Our place is to obey and go wherever we are sent, wherever God's Spirit leads. As we do what God tells us to do, we find that we are where He is—and that means we're always at home.

Obviously, I'm playing with the title of this book a bit. But I love, love, love that home is not only where God sends us, but also where He takes us. He is with us wherever He tells us to go. And because we're His children, that's what makes any place He leads us to our home.

Beloved, Heavenly Father, Home for My Heart and Soul, I am ever thankful You've made me Your child. As You lead me all over this world, help me to remember my home is not really a physical place. Home is living in loving obedience to You. Wherever You want me is where I want to be. In Your presence, I am home. Amen.

Acknowledgments

Thank You, Jesus, for everything! Without You, there'd be no life, no family to love, no friends to make, no world to explore, no book to write, no Truth to share. You give existence meaning—I love You!

Thank you, Mike, for believing in me and in this idea and for wanting to see me succeed. You put just enough pressure on your quiet wife to get these words out there.

Thank you, Justin and Bridget, Alex, and Seth, for making this life adventure so much more exciting! I can't imagine a world without any of you. Thank you, also, for letting God lead as you begin to seek and establish homes of your own. May He always bless your efforts as you strive to honor Him.

Thank you, Mom and Dad, for willingly letting our family go wherever God has led. Though He still hasn't chosen to lead us back toward you, you've always encouraged us to follow Him.

To Jim and to Pat, thank you for raising one truly amazing man to be my husband. For as long as we live, home is where God sends *us*. I'm so thankful God led me to Mike.

To all the friends I've made through military chapels and in PWOC (Protestant Women of the Chapel), thank you for your prayers and encouraging words as I've pursued this dream. I've read that writers need to have ideal readers in mind. You have been mine! May God bless you with contentment and a home in His presence wherever He leads.

Janet Benlien Reeves is an Army chaplain's wife, an empty-nest mom, and an author. She enjoys leading small group Bible studies and teaching others about the God she loves and His perfect plan for their lives. She holds a bachelor's degree in Christian education from Point Loma Nazarene University. Since they've been married, she and her husband have moved eleven times and have lived in eight states and the Netherlands. They have three grown sons and a precious daughter-in-law.

Visit Janet at her website: *WildflowerFaith.com*.

Made in the USA
Middletown, DE
17 April 2015